The Story
of
Oban Lifeboat

Willie Melville

Pen Press

First published in Great Britain by Pen Press is an
Imprint of Indepenpress Publishing Ltd
25 Eastern Place
Brighton
BN2 1GJ

ISBN 978-1-907172-11-3

Printed and bound in the UK

A catalogue record of this book is available from
the British Library

Cover design Jacqueline Abromeit
Photography Tony Hardley www.scotphoto.com

This book is dedicated to my wife, Margaret, who, over the past 45 years or so, has supported me in every way including in my lifeboat activities where she willingly and cheerfully accepted the occasional upsets which go hand-in-hand with being a member of the Lifeboat "family".

The Author is extremely grateful to the following parties for their generosity in the sponsorship of this book:

Donald MacKenzie, MacKenzie Interiors, Oban
Robbie Anderson, Hannah's Newsagents, Oban
Ian Cleaver, Highland Heritage, Dalmally
Ian Wallace, Nancy Black Chandlers, Oban
Oban Rotary Club
The Oban Times Limited
Ardfern Yacht Centre Limited
Maclean Marine Tuition, Aros Ard, Oban
Oban Lifeboat Crew
Maclean Marine Services, Machrie, Oban
Aggregate Industries (UK) Ltd, Glensanda
Mathesons Furnishings, Oban
Blairish Restorations Ltd
T Barbour Limited
Aulay Dunn, Oban
Oban Marina, Kerrera
Royal Highland Yacht Club
David Webster, Oban
Matrix Computers, Oban
Oban & Lorn Tourism Association
Ardoran Marine
Clyde Cruising Club Seamanship & Pilotage Trust

The net profits from the sale of this book will be donated to the RNLI.

Contents

PREFACE

In the long and distinguished history of the Royal National Lifeboat Institution (the RNLI), founded in 1824, a lifeboat station that is 36 years old at the time of writing can be considered a mere fledgling. It is remarkable, however, that, within 26 years of its founding, Oban Lifeboat had achieved, in one year, over 100 services – a record for a "one-boat" station.

Just how this progress was achieved and maintained, it is hoped will be shown throughout the remainder of this book, embracing both the "highs" and "lows" which affect all stations from time to time. The various services mentioned represent a mere fraction of the total number of launches but it is hoped that they might give a flavour of the variety of "shouts" to which Oban lifeboats respond.

A few of the detailed explanations given may draw comments from lifeboatmen of "teaching granny to suck eggs" but it is hoped that non-sailors may also read this book.

The term "honorary secretary" is used frequently throughout and, for the sake of clarity, it must be said that it does not refer to a secretary only in the correspondence sense. The honorary secretary, colloquially known as the "hon sec", apart from dealing with correspondence, is the principal launching authority and, generally, the "boss" of the station. The post of hon sec was re-named lifeboat operations manager around 2003 but it is likely that we shall hear of "hon secs" until almost an entire generation of lifeboatmen have passed on.

CHAPTER I

1972-1978

Setting Up

The setting up of a new lifeboat station from a standing start does not happen overnight. During 1971 and early 1972 the RNLI weighed up a number of factors affecting the sea area around Oban – the marine accident statistics over a period of years, the increase in leisure boating, the existence of a commercial fishing fleet (albeit in decline) and that the nearest lifeboat stations were at Port Askaig, Islay (50 miles to the south) and at Mallaig (60 miles to the north west).

The outcome was their decision to place a small "inshore" lifeboat (ILB) at Oban and a small "steering" committee was set up under the guidance of the then staff coxswain, the late Tom Beattie and the then district inspector, Harry Teare. This committee included the late Archie MacAllister, extremely knowledgeable about local waters, Captain Norman MacLeod, teacher of navigation at Oban High School, Lake Falconer, Oban solicitor and yachtsman, Donnie Currie, Oban boat-builder, the late John Ramage, hotelier and experienced sailor and Willie Melville, former crewmember of Helensburgh Inshore Lifeboat.

Their immediate task was the selection of individuals to fill the various posts necessary in the operation of a lifeboat station. Most important of these is the position of hon sec – who has operational control of the station, backed up by two or three deputy launching authorities (DLA). The first hon sec was Norman Budge, piermaster, whose home was on the South Pier and adjacent to the new lifeboat's proposed mooring – an ideal situation. DLA appointed were Norman MacLeod, Lake Falconer and Donnie Currie.

The ILB (Inshore Lifeboat) Years

On the 5th day of the 5th month in 1972, the MacLachlan-class inshore lifeboat, appropriately numbered A505, was launched into Oban Bay and, under the eagle eye of Inspector Harry Teare, a few likely helmsmen were put through their paces in handling her. A crew "pool" of some 11 men was created, the boat requiring a crew of two for a call-out – or a "shout" as a service is colloquially known in the Institution. (The minimum crew officially became three before the MacLachlan was replaced at Oban.) Inshore lifeboats, or inshore rescue boats as they were initially named, did not provide year-round cover, their "season" varying from station to station and in Oban's case, settled down as a March/April arrival from the depot in Poole or the Isle of Wight and a return to depot in September/October.

Mooring

A mooring was laid for her in the south-east corner of Oban Bay just off the then wooden pier used by fishing boats in greater numbers than, sadly, we see now. The lifeboat lay facing approximately NNW, a stern line maintaining her in this position. Boarding by the three-man crew was with an 8 ft inflatable dinghy donated to the station by the late Bill Crerar, a good friend of the Lifeboat Service and, at that time, a local architect and hotelier.

Shore Facilities

Somewhere had to be found near the mooring in which to store not only the dinghy and oars but also lifejackets, foul-weather gear, fuel and a writing desk of some sort. "Basic facilities" was how the committee described their needs and this exactly what they got!

All who remember the South Pier in those days will recall the row of three tin-roofed sheds on the west side of the pier and running approximately at right angles to the road. The most northerly of these was occupied by Vale Engineering whose proprietor then was Ken Coffee while the other two were used as storehouses – all three were owned by the Council. Initially, the most southerly unit was rented by the RNLI from the Council and, from this un-prepossessing tin shed, its walls running with water from the road at times, operations began.

Maroons

Calling out the crew for a shout was done by the traditional method of firing two rockets (known as maroons) by hand. These rockets were set off by the launching authority, usually the hon sec, from the "shed" – correctly the "station" – and soared to about 1000/1200 ft before they exploded with a tremendous bang heard by the whole population including, hopefully, the crew. Occasionally, a member of the crew engaged in working, say, in the engine-room of a fishing boat might not hear the maroons or, at best, hear only a muffled noise. In this regard, in one shout, a crewmember working in his basement responded to what he thought were maroons and shot off to the station in the car hotly pursued by his wife on foot waving a towel and shouting that she had merely closed a door in the house above him, rather heavily. He returned home shortly thereafter having found no-one at the station and boat swinging quietly to her mooring.

As a back-up to maroons, a "phone-round" was set in place by Dr Gordon Murchison, the station's honorary medical advisor (HMA). This was known as an "explosive" phone around and every member who heard the signal would phone two other crewmembers (more often than not the married men delegated the job to their wives) and say "launch!" Thus, every crewman made and received two calls assuming everyone heard the maroons! They are now things of the past, having been superseded by individual pagers.

On Service

Regular exercises were carried out to increase the proficiency of all the boat handlers and within three weeks of the boat being placed on service, the first real "shout" took place. Little did the three youngsters who set off from Ganavan in their parents' sailing dinghy on Sunday, 24 May 1972, realise that they were about to become the first entry in Oban lifeboat's service records. A stiff easterly wind was blowing and it soon became apparent that the dinghy and her occupants were unable to turn for home. The ILB, A505, crewed by Patrick Maclean and Douglas MacQueen, was launched and, in the nick of time, caught up with the dinghy to take the children aboard before they would almost certainly have foundered on the Creag Islands.

Before the boat was taken off station for the winter in October, she had launched on service a further ten times. All 11 services were to show the new station, its officials and crewmembers, just how varied they might expect their work to be, including as they did – people swept away and cut off, a power-boat swamped, an overdue rowing boat, false alarms, a cabin cruiser on fire and a hoax call. They resulted, variously, in the saving of the persons involved, in others coping and, in two cases, the sad return of a body.

In the spring of 1973, a brand new MacLachlan-class ILB, A 511, replaced the original. The sum of £5000 towards the cost of this boat was generously donated by the North British Trust Hotels and handed over by the then chairman of the trust, the late Norris D Beith, at a gathering in their Oban Bay Hotel. This proved to be the first of several gifts of one kind or another to Oban Lifeboat by the trust.

The new boat's first service was to search for overdue divers in conditions of thick fog patches, not a hazard often encountered in the Oban area. They were found in due course and escorted back to Oban none the worse but making the point that they had seen the same vessel pass them twice, failing to spot them on both occasions (a reminder to all of us, perhaps, that, on searches in fog, it is advisable to switch off one's engine periodically and just listen for sounds of any kind).

Around this time there developed, unfortunately, what might be described as a "rift" between the hon sec, the late Norman Budge, and the crew. Differences of opinion regarding how and by whom the boat was manned was the root of the problem. Sadly, matters deteriorated further when the Press got wind of it. When one newspaper carried an alleged reference by the then hon sec to "my fair weather crew members" and the inference that either THEY resigned or HE did, the bubble burst, as it were, and the entire crew held a meeting attended only by themselves and the chairman. It took little time for a unanimous decision to be reached that NO crew members would resign. This outcome was conveyed to Mr Budge and, in July 1973, he was succeeded by one of the deputy launching authorities, Captain Norman MacLeod, principal teacher of navigation at Oban High School, who held the post for the next 29 years until his retiral in 2002.

Calls of all kinds continued during each succeeding season, these averaging ten per year and falling into categories described variously in RNLI parlance as, perhaps, Vessel Overdue, Stranding, Man Overboard, Out of Fuel, Steering Failure, Vessel Meeting Adverse Conditions, Capsize and many more. The RNLI has its own vocabulary of phrases also for the outcome of shouts, probably the most welcome one to both lifeboat crew and survivors being "Persons Saved and Craft Brought In".

Another one which states quite simply "Gave Help" may sometimes embrace great activity on the part of the lifeboat ranging from putting a crew member aboard the casualty to assist in raising the anchor or to repair some electrical/mechanical fault. Occasionally the lifeboat crewman will remain aboard while the lifeboat escorts the casualty to port.

In June 1974, a doctor, temporarily working as a "locum" in the area, required to be taken to the Isle of Mull long after ferries had ceased to run. He was not used to boats and was clearly apprehensive of the trip in the lifeboat. In the event, he coped admirably with the sea journey but told us next day that the ride in the police car thereafter had been hair-raising!

One service which, with hindsight, was a pointer to the future took place on 24 June when the small 18-ft *MacLachlan* secured a tow on a 16-ton motor yacht, with five persons on board, which was without power and drifting just 350yds off the Duart shore. Fortunately the wind was light southerly and, without requiring to put great strain on the engines and hull of the ILB, she towed the casualty at slow speed to Oban.

One of the services furthest from the station took place on 11 September 1974 when two fishing boats, the *Maighdean Hearrach* and the *Ros Guill* failed to negotiate Ardmore Point on the north coast of Mull and ran hard aground virtually under Ardmore Light – BOTH of them! The *MacLachlan* was launched at 0422 hours reaching the stricken vessels at 0635. On scene also were a few other fishing boats unable to assist due to their draft and a falling tide. The ILB, however, was able to run their lines to the stranded vessels to await high tide in the afternoon when an attempt to tow the casualties off would be made.

During a lull in operations, the ILB crew nipped round to Tobermory to have some breakfast – only to realise that, having left home in some haste at 4am, none of them had any cash! The problem was solved, however, when the banker in the crew met one of his customers, Ewen Kennedy, the Oban butcher, delivering meat and borrowed £5 from him! That fiver bought the three men their breakfast, paid their ferry fares home and left just enough for a cup of coffee on the way – what price inflation?! All three crewmembers of the ILB had commitments later in the day and a relief crew was sent out to Craignure on the ferry to take over to stand-by at the re-floating attempt. Initially, matters went well, the *Ros Guill* coming off but her hull had suffered severely and she sank within minutes. The *Maighdean Hearrach* with a badly damaged keel was left on the Point for the time being. She lay there for many years disintegrating and today almost nothing identifiable is visible.

In October 1974 a small plane, with two persons aboard, failed to take off from Connel Airstrip crashing into the sea off Saulmore. The ILB was launched to the scene and spent the following seven hours searching for the passenger who had been seen in the water just after the plane came down as well as assisting divers and other rescue teams in their attempts to check the sunken plane. The passenger was found to be missing and the pilot found dead on board – his body was brought back to Oban by the lifeboat and handed over to the police. No trace was found of the passenger.

By 1976 the Remarks Box in some reports of services submitted routinely by the hon sec, Norman MacLeod and his deputy launching authorities were revealing a trend – this indicating that, on certain services, the *MacLachlan* was being stretched to her limits. This did not always refer to her ability to cope with heavy seas but also to the difficulties the crew were experiencing in keeping the VHF handset dry and in using a chart in some conditions.

On one service to assist a 20-ft launch with one person on board, adrift in Craignure Bay, Isle of Mull on 6 October 1976, the crew reported that they were encountering seas of about 15 ft just outside Oban Bay and were sheltering at the north end of the Isle of Kerrera. Norman MacLeod's wise decision to re-call the lifeboat was the right one. The casualty landed ashore safely at Craignure.

Another of the services pointing to the need for a "bigger" lifeboat took place on 27 July 1977 when the MacLachlan not only sailed 14 miles to the scene at Port Appin but towed back to Oban a motor-cruiser with four persons aboard.

On 9 April 1978 the ILB was launched in response to red flares seen in Loch Spelve, some 10 miles from the station. The wind was NNW Force 7/8 and she was escorted by the FV *Strathisla* but who was limited by draught for entry to the loch. The casualties were found to be two charter boats dragging anchor – in one case the anchor had broken leaving only the shank. Using the lifeboat's own anchor, both were secured off the north shore and a family of three taken aboard the ILB who returned to mouth of the loch where the

Strathisla had remained and whose skipper, using his radar, conned the lifeboat clear – this assistance was invaluable. The family was transferred to the fishing vessel and later taken to hospital for observation. Once more the hon sec's comments in the return of service were pertinent – "It is to be hoped that any future lifeboat would be fitted with a reliable radar as navigational aids in this area are non-existent." *(Navaids much improved now – author – 12/08.)*

All in all, it was obvious that the RNLI Committee of Management had to reconsider the requirements for lifeboat cover in the Oban area. The inshore boat had done all that was expected of her and more – but she had not been designed to cope with some of the more severe conditions encountered even in the relatively sheltered waters of the Firth of Lorne, far less in the sea area to the south west and along the rugged south coast of the Isle of Mull. Their decision to place an all-weather lifeboat at Oban was welcomed by committee and crew alike. The reason for visits by Sir Charles McGrigor, chairman of the Scottish Lifeboat Council and a member of the Institution's Committee of Management, between September 1977 and May 1978, accompanied by Cdr Bruce Cairns, chief of operations or by Captain N Dixon, Director of the RNLI, now became clear!

One tradition established during the early days of Oban's first lifeboat and which is maintained to this day is the annual crew dinner. These memorable evenings were, initially, held in Soroba House Hotel – where else? – for proprietor David Hutcheson and his wife Edyth had been good friends and supporters of Oban Lifeboat from the start. Many of the original crew will remember returning from one of the first shouts and finding a 40 oz bottle of whisky sitting on the desk – no indication of the donor and Davie will probably still deny that it was he who put it there.

Until the arrival of the all-weather boat, these affairs were all-male, crew-only and many a time, when a waitress entered the room, Jim Kirkham who had become the crew story-teller, had to stop in mid-sentence to save the poor lassie's blushes! It must also be said that crew dinners were paid for out of the crew fund – this being where all service and exercise payments were deposited by the crew. In 1972 the service payment to each man was £1.50 for the first two hours (the majority of shouts were completed within this time) and the fund grew steadily but, despite David Hutcheson's "substantial discount" was pretty well wiped out at these dinners.

There was, however, usually enough in the kitty to buy the odd present for any crewmember leaving or getting married – this frequently being a painting by local artist Bob MacCulloch, a dentist by profession. Bob's superb seascapes adorn many a home in the town, and further afield. Many of them show a lifeboat – by request. In later years, these dinners became much more genteel affairs with the ladies also invited.

Sadly, the venue had to be changed when fire gutted Soroba House in 1979 and the function has had several homes since then.

CHAPTER II

1978-1981

The Watson Years

The all-weather lifeboat arrived in Oban in August 1978 under the command of Commander Mike Vlasto, divisional inspector and with coxswain/mechanic designate, John Patrick Maclean and experienced MN officer, Graham MacQueen aboard. Much familiarisation of the boat and machinery was able to be carried out on the passage from Mashford's boat yard, Plymouth while the experience of Tom Peebles, divisional engineer, and Skegness coxswain, Ken Holland was also on hand. The whole passage could be described as one continuous exercise.

She was the 42-ft Watson-class boat the *Watkin Williams* formerly the Moelfre (Anglesey) lifeboat. Powered by twin 48 HP Gardner diesel engines, she was capable of 8.25 knots – with the wind "up her kilt" some would say. Clearly this is a far cry from today's lifeboat speeds of 25+ knots but seldom was it necessary to reduce that speed despite bad weather. The need to reach casualties in faster times, however, were both necessary and, with the development of technology, also possible – as we shall see. Unlike some earlier powered open lifeboats, this Watson had a "roof" over the steering position under which the crew could shelter when under way. The engine room occupied much of the hull and was accessed through a hatch just forward of the wheel. Since a fatal accident some years previously when two mechanics succumbed to fumes while in a lifeboat engine room, no one was allowed to remain in there for longer than was necessary to carry out essential duties. The only other space below decks was a small cabin in the bow which housed the MF radio, a Neil Robertson stretcher and provided survivor accommodation. Crew numbered seven in total with Pat Maclean, coxswain/mechanic (appointed 1.12.78) and David Graham, second coxswain.

The *Watkin Williams* arrived at the station with a highly commendable past record, her last coxswain being Dick Evans, BEM who had been awarded a bar to his gold medal for the rescue of ten members of the crew of the Greek freighter *Nafsiporus* in December 1966. The freighter had drifted without power across the Irish Sea in a north westerly Force 11. Both Holyhead and Moelfre lifeboats were launched to her assistance in horrendous conditions, both coxswains receiving a gold medal and all members of both crews being awarded either silver or bronze medals.

The *Watkin Williams'* first service at Oban took place on 26 August 1978 and was a joint one with the ILB. The cause was a crewmember of a yacht in the anchorage at Dunstaffnage having suffered a stroke. The HMA was dispatched in the ILB in order that he might administer quickly what treatment he thought fit and so that the crew could assess the possibility of landing the patient at the Marine Laboratory pier for transfer to an ambulance.

Much training was necessary to bring the crew up to the required levels of navigation, seamanship, first-aid and many more aspects of what, in the all-weather boat, was now possible as well as necessary. The coxswain/mechanic, Pat Maclean, ex Merchant Navy, taught seamanship and navigation during the regular Monday evening meetings of the crew as did the HMA, Gordon Murchison in respect of first-aid and CPR (cardio pulmonary resuscitation). On some evenings, half of the crew exercised the boat at sea while the remainder poured over charts or listened to "Murch" in the shed.

The "shed" was now over twice its original size, the Council having leased to the Institution the unit next door and the crew having re-furbished it to a very high standard indeed. This was achieved not only by using the payments (such as they were) for services and exercises but also by felling trees and splitting the wood into bundles of firewood, which were sold.

Wilson Scott and Sydney ("Twirly") Thomson ran discos to raise further funds.

On 10 September 1978 the *Watkin Williams* cooperated with the customs patrol vessel *Challenge* in assisting an 18-ft fibre-glass boat adrift with engine trouble some 8 miles SW of Oban, four persons aboard. On scene the customs vessel was standing by while a member from the casualty swam out to her with a messenger line as the lobster boat was now ashore. *Challenge* towed her off, her engineer effecting temporary repairs and she was able to return to Oban escorted by the lifeboat.

In June 1979, the *Watkin Williams* went to the Clyde for her annual refit and was replaced by the relief lifeboat *Southern Africa*, a 51-ft Barnett-class. The relief boat did only one service during her time at the station (from which she was recalled as another vessel had coped) but the crew was to meet up with her again in November 1981.

With the *Watkins Williams* back on station, the usual variety of services took place. The Firth of Lorne and the Sound of Mull being superb skin-diving territory, it is inevitable that many services by any Oban lifeboat will be to divers or diving tenders. The first such incident attended by an Oban ALB (accompanied by the ILB) took place on 16 September 1979 when two divers were reported overdue to resurface by 45 minutes. Due to worsening weather conditions and decreasing visibility, both boats were launched at 1444 and 1500 hours respectively, the *Watson* taking with her three volunteer divers from the party. A Sea King SAR (Search and Rescue) helicopter from Prestwick also joined the search for which the original point of reference was off Duart Castle. At 1625 hours the ALB reported diving gear on the shore and two persons were sighted at Camus Gorm. The helicopter made unsuccessful attempts to winch the two men and the ILB closed the shore to pick them up and transfer them to the *Watson*. They had been located 4.5 miles away from the expected surfacing position.

In mid-November, two men who had taken a 14-ft boat with outboard to the Creag Islands were reported overdue home at

1927 hours. They were believed to have oars and ONE lifejacket. The lifeboat was launched at 1940 hours and about half a mile north of Maiden Island, fired a white parachute flare both to illuminate the area the men might be in and to let them know (hopefully) that somebody was looking for them. At the Creag Islands the lifeboat sighted a dinghy on the shore and saw flames in the entrance to a small cave whereupon she dropped anchor and kedged back into the beach. By 2032 hours the men were aboard, the gear recovered, their dinghy taken in tow and the lifeboat headed for home. With hindsight, the decision to take the men off the island, despite their cave and fire, was very much the right one, temperatures during that night having fallen to below freezing and one of the two was elderly.

The year 1980 saw service launches total 17 – this time nine by the inshore boat and eight by the AWL (all-weather lifeboat) – sometimes together.

Just after midnight on 17 May the ILB was launched to investigate the cause of two sightings of red flares in the area between Loch Don and the south end of the island of Kerrera. The lifeboat was joined in the search by the motor launch *Dirk*, which searched the west side of Kerrera while the former went south into the Sound of Kerrera. Coastguard now reported that a small speedboat was missing from Oban with two inebriated persons aboard and, shortly after, the ILB sighted a white flare in the Sound of Kerrera area and replied with a white parachute flare to illuminate the area – this showed nothing. After some four hours the search was suspended, nothing having been found. It was believed later that two persons were interviewed by Oban Police and had admitted to taking a 16-ft boat with outboard motor and firing two red flares and one white parachute flare. The "down-side" for the rescue boats, of course, was the not insignificant cost of fuel, flares and lost sleep.

Both lifeboats were launched on 20 August 1980 following the report of a missing diver who had been diving in a disused tidal quarry at Easdale. The ILB was on scene before the *Watson* and began a systematic search until the police, having considered all the known facts, decided to "net" the quarry entrance and call in a naval diving team, the lifeboats returning to station.

Four days later, both boats were again launched to search for an overdue 10-ft dinghy with two persons aboard. The lifeboats slipped their moorings just before 10pm and, with no last known location of the casualty, the search area was a wide one. With no sightings by 0100 hours the search was suspended until 0600 when a Sea King helicopter joined the search team. During the previous evening's search, the ILB encountered problems with her starboard engine and was on restricted service until she was withdrawn altogether before noon – a mechanic was sent from base and the *MacLachlan* was repaired and ready for service before nightfall. All areas having been combed without success, the search was called off at 1720 hours.

It seems so unfair – and it happens quite often – that a vessel going to the aid of another, herself gets into difficulties. And it happened on 12 September 1980 when that fine Scots actor, Ian Cuthbertson, in his Fifer motor cruiser *Sea Laughter*, went to the assistance of a yacht adrift in the Sound of Kerrera in a WNW Force 7 wind. In such a wind it is not surprising that *Sea Laughter* herself grounded at Dungallan only some two or three cables "round the corner" from the lifeboat station and the *Watkin Williams* was launched at 2050 hours. The tide was already on the ebb and several unsuccessful attempts were made to tow her off, the decision being reached to return to station and make another attempt on a making tide in the morning. At 0700 hours the following day, *Sea Laughter* having survived her night ashore comfortably, the lifeboat launched again and Coxswain Maclean decided to drop anchor and pay out cable until he was in a position to connect the tow in order that he would have better control at "float-off". At 0840 hours, with the assistance of the ML *Dirk* (which Mr Cuthbertson had arranged the previous evening), *Sea Laughter* refloated. The yacht that she initially went to assist was recovered by her owners.

To quote from the original title of the service, "...for the Preservation of Life from Shipwreck", it has to be remembered that every service a lifeboat does is not DIRECTLY achieving the aim but preventing the potential loss of life at sea. So it was on 22 September 1980 when, while on exercise, Oban piermaster advised the lifeboat that a motor-cruiser was adrift off Ganavan and could be a danger to shipping and to keep a look-out. Within an hour the lifeboat had located the vessel and took it in tow to Oban, where the police informed the owner who was asked to "collect". Had the boat adrift with no lights collided with, say, a small dinghy with persons aboard, life may well have been lost.

At the beginning of February 1981, there occurred one of those shouts that "puzzled" the hon sec and coxswain as the reports came through. At 0139 hours on 2 February 1981 coastguard reported that a motor-cruiser with ten persons aboard had grounded in Loch Aline and requested tow. The car-ferry *Rhum*, moored at Loch Aline, was unable to locate the casualty. The car ferry, *Pioneer* and a fishing boat were all asked to keep a lookout and the lifeboat was launched at 0218 hours. About an hour later the casualty radioed "am afloat – making for Tobermory" – no answer to the coastguard's request for her position. Between 0400 hours and 0420 hours the lifeboat fired various flares, which were "not seen" by the casualty. The lifeboat was then recalled and the "pan pan" cancelled.

However, at 0930 next morning, coastguard reported the casualty aground in Loch Don but survivors safely ashore – Loch Don is, of course, some 9 miles SE of Loch Aline! At 1455 hours the *Watkin Williams* launched again to stand-by at the attempt to refloat the casualty but, despite numerous attempts, she remained firmly on the rock, only coming off on a high tide next day. Conditions during most of this service were bad, visibility in rain squalls poor – leading Captain MacLeod again to make a plea for radar.

Another service involving both boats occurred on 25 April 1981 in response to a mayday call at 0329 hours from a fishing vessel with three persons aboard in the Sound of Mull. She had struck rocks off Lochaline, was making water and urgently required a pump. The pump from the lightship *Fingal* was put aboard the ILB and taken at speed to the casualty while the *Watkin Williams* sailed with a second pump from the fire brigade, it too being put aboard the casualty by the ILB. The incident ended happily, the fishing vessel, escorted by the lifeboat, making Oban under her own power at 0630 hours.

At the end of June both lifeboats, an SAR helicopter, the Marine Laboratory's *Calanus* and other vessels searched unsuccessfully for a missing diver in the area of Heather Island, Sound of Kerrera. A diving team from the *Calanus* searched the underwater cave on Heather Island, coastguard personnel combed the shore and the boats carried out numerous searches of the whole area but, tragically, to no avail.

There was a similarly sad outcome when the inshore lifeboat, searching for a diver who had failed to re-surface from an inspection of his creels in Loch Feochan on 28 August, found him tangled in a marker-buoy rope below the surface.

In early September 1981, a 16-ton fishing vessel on fire saw the *Watkin Williams*, with a fire-pump aboard, heading for one of several positions reported, ranging from "10 miles NW of Corriebhreacan" to "NxE 7 miles from Loch Buie – nearly reciprocal! In the event, the position was academic to the lifeboat because she was recalled. The vessel on fire was under tow by another fishing boat to which the casualty's three crewmen had been transferred. After a report that the fire seemed to be spreading, the tow was released and the towing vessel stood off and warned other vessels also to keep clear. The lifeboat was then recalled.

The banker in the crew was on board that day, having glanced at his desk diary on hearing the maroons and saw that his only appointment that afternoon was with a customer who was also a member of the lifeboat crew and would almost certainly also be unable to make the meeting. And so it was – for, after turning for home, the pair retired to the foredeck and in brilliant sunshine held their discussion as planned. It was perhaps just as well, as this same banker didn't want to lose his customers, that the story of how he got to the station that day wasn't made public until after his retirement. With no car nearby, he decided to run to the lifeboat but, on reaching Argyll Square, instead of taking the shortest route he ran round the roundabout as if he was driving!

While the ILB was on exercise in Oban Bay on 15 October 1981 she was asked to investigate a report of an "orange" flare seen by a fishing boat and thought be in the Lynn of Morven. Nothing was found but coastguard considered it might have been the after-burn from low-flying military aircraft known to have been in the area at the time. This has been the reason given for similar reports over the years and, certainly, on seeing such aircraft from certain angles, one might interpret after-burn as flares.

The *Dorothy and Philip Constant*

Several comments over previous months by Norman MacLeod, the hon sec, on returns of services, saying "radar would have been helpful" were obviously taken on board by the Institution and, in November 1981, the 42-ft Watson-class lifeboat, *Dorothy and Philip Constant* replaced the *Watkin Williams*.

They were, in fact, sister-ships but for one factor – the new boat was fitted with radar. The "swap" took place on Armistice Sunday under the surveillance of the inspector, Mike Vlasto, who, at 11am precisely, brought the crew to attention facing the town and paid respects to the fallen by observing two minutes' silence.

The *Dorothy and Philip Constant* had formerly been the Shoreham Harbour lifeboat from 1963 – a "housed" boat launching down a slipway. Protected from the elements, therefore, she was in superb condition and to maintain a moored boat similarly is a hard act to follow but the Oban coxswain/mechanic and his crew met the challenge extremely well.

By now, the 51-ft Barnett-class relief lifeboat, *Southern Africa*, referred to in June 1979, had been sold out of service by the Institution to the harbour authority in Valparaiso, Chile. She lay at Rosneath in the Gareloch and Oban coxswain Patrick Maclean, was given the task of arranging a passage crew with orders to sail for Liverpool on 20 November 1981. However, 20 November was the date of Oban Lifeboat dinner dance and, since the passage crew was composed totally of Oban crew, the departure was delayed until 21 November. They duly left on the 21st under dire warnings from HQ in Poole not to be late in arriving in Liverpool since the freighter transporting the lifeboat expected delivery by Monday, 23rd!

Dinner dance over, the passage crew headed for the Gareloch and, against all predictions, arrived there safely and on time and made ready for sea. Good progress was made down the North Channel in a brisk north-westerly breeze. During the night, Gordon Murchison decided to make coffee using the boat's only means of boiling water, a primus stove. After what seemed an eternity, the coffee was produced only to be spat out as "foul" by everyone except "Murch" who pronounced it "OK". When dawn broke all was revealed when the water container from which the coffee had been made was seen to be marked "Anti Freeze".

The wind was still freshening as dawn broke and a decision was made to put in "for a while" at Port St Mary, Isle of Man. With time in hand, the hospitality of the Port St Mary Lifeboat crew was too good to refuse and 5am on the 23rd seeing the *Southern Africa* leave Port St Mary for Liverpool, her intended day of arrival still well in hand. Clearing the shelter of Port St Mary, however, she encountered a big head-sea and, after a particularly nasty one ripped the cover off the rope locker, Coxswain Maclean decided to return to Port St Mary to await an improvement in the weather. On telephoning HQ to advise the position, the duty officer replied, "Don't worry old chap, the freighter shipping your lifeboat is a week late."! The lifeboat was delivered next day and duly took up duty in Valparaiso soon thereafter.

The first service performed on 9 November by the *Dorothy and Philip Constant* was to act as OSC (on scene commander) in a search for an overdue diver in the Dubh Sgeir area SW of Kerrera. Other vessels also involved were *Gratitude, Pass of Chisholm, Barcadale,* RN diving tender *Ixworth* and Cal Mac's *Glen Sannox.* A Sea King helicopter was also airborne from Prestwick. The diver was spotted by the *Glen Sannox* and picked up by a boat lowered by *Ixworth* – all was well. The new (to Oban Lifeboat) radar proved invaluable – although it was daylight, it assisted in maintaining search patterns amongst the many craft involved.

Of the seven services performed by the *Dorothy and Philip Constant* while at Oban, probably the most unusual so far the coxswain and crew are concerned was on 11 January 1982 when they became "ice-bound". The lifeboat was already on exercise when reports of red flares in the Loch Don/Loch Spelve area of Mull were received. Further white flares were seen and, having drawn a blank in Loch Don, the lifeboat turned south for Loch Spelve. In the short run down to Loch Spelve, the very loud noise of aircraft propellers apparently just ahead was heard by all aboard and when Wilson Scott smartly shone the searchlight upwards, he caught the unmistakable sight of a Hercules aircraft flying low over the lifeboat. This ought to have given a clue to what was going on. However, the lifeboat entered Loch Spelve, negotiated the "nasty bit", which was not marked in those days, and shortly afterwards, ran into ice!

The boat seemed to rise over the "lip" of the frozen area and settle in a hole surrounded by ice. Breaking the ice with boat hooks, the lifeboat was turned round and headed back for the open sea. At this point, the emergency supplies of Mars Bars were opened – only to find that the temperature had turned them into almost inedible steel bars! Nevertheless, none was returned to the locker!

On returning to Oban the waterline paintwork was seen to be cut right through to the bare wood, such is the effect of ice shards. The search, of course, found nothing and only later did we learn that it was thought the SAS was exercising on

Mull that night! A quiet "word" with the emergency services in advance would not have gone amiss.

Police requested lifeboat assistance in the search for a woman missing from her home in Connel on 21 February 1982 so, with a crew of eight and two inflatable dinghies aboard, the *Dorothy and Philip Constant* headed for Loch Etive. Crewmen were landed on the several small islands in the area both inside and outside Loch Etive and the mainland shores were also searched before the lifeboat moved into Ardmucknish Bay to investigate the beach there. The Dunstaffnage to Ganavan shore was also covered but with no success even after these extensive searches over two days.

Some members of a party of nine canoeists working the Falls of Lora on 26 February got into difficulties resulting, once a head-count was done, in there still being one 14-year-old boy missing. The lifeboat was launched immediately and the offer of assistance by the crew of a Northern Lighthouse Board helicopter, on her way back to Peterhead, accepted straight away. At 1426 hours the helicopter reported "...have what appears to be a body below" and the lifeboat, with the HMA on the crew, took the casualty aboard at 1430 – still alive but unconscious and extremely hypothermic. The ambulance was re-directed to the Marine Laboratory pontoon where the youngster was landed within minutes and taken to hospital accompanied by the HMA.

That lucky now-40-year-old will, for ever, have cause to be immensely grateful to, first of all, the helicopter pilots who, with the huge visual advantage of height, located him so quickly and secondly to the lifeboat HMA, Dr Gordon Murchison for his treatment during the period between taking him aboard the lifeboat and getting him to hospital.

A medical evacuation from the island of Kerrera on 12 April 1982 was that of Mr Archie MacAllister, one of the members of the steering committee (referred to on page 3 of this book.) He had suffered a heart attack at his Kerrera cottage and was transferred on a stretcher across the large boarding boat out to the Watson – surely not the most comfortable of journeys. This was the last effective service performed by the *Dorothy and Philip Constant* before the Brede 33-02 became the station lifeboat. The *Dorothy and Philip Constant,* which was the last 42-ft Watson-class lifeboat built for the RNLI, is now the flagship of a Norfolk RYA training centre and sails under the name *Constance of Blakeney.*

Since 1972 the sturdy little 18-ft *MacLachlan* had been launched a total of 63 times and credited with saving 12 lives. Following the arrival of the all-weather boat in 1978, officially as back-up to the ILB, the *MacLachlan* had remained on "summer-only" duty and continued to be launched on her own when the smaller, faster, shallower-draft boat was considered to be appropriate. On other occasions, when her draft and speed were critical to the service, she accompanied the all-weather boat and they carried out joint services five times. Including these, Oban inshore lifeboats were launched 99 times in total.

A 511 was eventually "retired" in 1982, her last service being on 9 April when she ferried the station's HMA, Dr Gordon Murchison to the island of Kerrera to treat a four-year-old girl. This valedictory service turned out to be a "double", since, when lying off awaiting the doctor's return, the boat was requested to investigate the sound of an explosion further down the Sound of Kerrera – this turned out to be no more than a "thunder-flash" type flare used by divers, accidentally exploding nearer the surface than usual – it could be said that MacLachlan lifeboats at Oban went out with a bang.

CHAPTER III

1981-1989

The Brede Years (i)

From an 18-ft inshore lifeboat to a 42-ft Watson-class all-weather lifeboat with radar represented considerable progress for a new station but a further factor required to be addressed – the need for an increase in the speed with which the boat could reach a casualty. The Committee of Management was clearly aware of this too and it is a credit to the hon sec, coxswain and crew that, after only ten years, the first of a new class of lifeboat was placed at Oban – a "Brede".

The "Brede", classed as an intermediate lifeboat, was 33 ft in length and was fitted with two Caterpillar 3208 203 HP diesel engines. Her maximum speed was 18.6 knots.

She was not an "all-weather" boat and was limited to launching at night in winds no greater than Force 7 although it was inevitable that, at times, she would encounter much stronger winds than that. In such circumstances she behaved extremely well and never gave her coxswain and crew one moment of anxiety. Her donor, Mrs Ann Ritchie of the Isle of Man, had, with her late husband, already donated two lifeboats to the Institution – truly magnanimous gifts. Mrs Ritchie was Welsh, her late husband Scottish and had been in business on the Isle of Man.

This time the lifeboat was to be named *Ann Ritchie* and the gracious lady herself came north to christen her gift on Saturday, 7 May 1983. On the previous evening Mrs Ritchie entertained the crew and wives to dinner when the crew presented her with a painting (by Bob MacCulloch of course) of the new lifeboat together with a Caithness Glass bowl engraved with the *Ann Ritchie* at speed. This was, of course, before the ugly pier development spoiled the corner altogether for small boats and the lifeboat on that day was moored in the angle of the pier and shore. Several hundred invited guests were seated on the pier and the platform party, under the chairmanship of Lake Falconer, occupied a dais facing the boat. After the formalities of accepting the lifeboat and the blessing of the boat, Mrs Ritchie, accompanied by Divisional Inspector Mike Vlasto, pressed the button, which released the bottle of champagne to smash over the bow of the *Ann Ritchie*. By fair means or foul, a Ritchie "house" flag had been procured and was hoisted as Mrs Ritchie boarded "her" boat for a short sail round Oban Bay. Her house flag displayed the Welsh dragon, the Three Legs of Man and the Lion Rampant. At the same time, a Wessex helicopter of RAF Leuchars, flying a huge RNLI flag, circled the bay.

The social side of the day then began. Tea and buns at Oban High School, just after the naming ceremony and where Mrs Ritchie "cut the cake" (a splendid iced cake showing the *Ann Ritchie*), were followed by a buffet/dance in the evening at Soroba House Hotel where "mine host", David Hutcheson, produced a buffet which excelled even HIS very high standards – all of this is recorded on video in station archives.

Mrs Ritchie maintained an interest in "her" lifeboat for the rest of her life until she died on 16 April 1990. She had, however, left instructions that, on her death, the painting and the bowl referred to above be returned to Oban Lifeboat Station where, today, they are proudly displayed.

If some members of the fishing community had thought that this small lifeboat would be of little assistance to them (and some did) then the first two services performed by the Brede ought to have made them think again. The *Ann Ritchie*'s first service on 29 June 1982 was to a 55-ft fishing boat sailing for the fishing grounds and had run aground some 3 miles SW of the station. The FV *Alert* had failed to refloat her and the Brede was given the opportunity to attempt to haul her off. With the newfound power and manoeuvrability the lifeboat refloated the *Cawsand Bay* without difficulty.

Her next service, on 7 August, was to another fishing vessel, the *Boston Sea Hawk,* bound for Milford Haven from Mallaig and who had grounded on Oban's Corran Ledge. The master of the *Boston Sea Hawk* considered the attempt to tow her off as a "no hope" task, the vessel being 62 tons nett. The increased power of the lifeboat, however, succeeded in refloating the casualty. It must be said that a lifeboat coxswain will never attempt to haul a casualty off before ensuring that her master agrees and appreciates the possible damage to the vessel.

The new boat's third launch was to a very much smaller vessel – a sailing dinghy, in fact, off Ganavan. In a fresh westerly wind on 10 August, two Austrian visitors capsized their dinghy, which filled and drifted off leaving them stranded on Sgeir Eitich. On taking the two survivors aboard the Brede using her own inflatable, one was found to be badly chilled and an ambulance was requested to meet the lifeboat.

Having delivered the casualties to the ambulance, the lifeboat returned to Ganavan to pick up the dinghy and two lifeboat crewmen who had been left to recover it.

The Brede continued to justify her selection as Oban lifeboat when, next day, there occurred the first of the many medical evacuations she would carry out during her years at the station. A member of the crew of a yacht anchored in Loch Aline who was suffering from acute pulmonary oedema, required medical attention and, taking the HMA, the lifeboat landed him on the yacht from where the patient was taken aboard the Brede and thence to hospital. The patient had been speedily and comfortably conveyed to Oban in a way which would not have been possible by either the MacLachlan or the Watson.

The last service of the year by the *Ann Ritchie* in 1982 was to escort a 23-ft motor cruiser back to Oban after she had been reported overdue from a passage round Kerrera. She was located half way between Maiden Island and Lismore Light but showing no lights and it was suggested that she follow the lifeboat into Oban Bay, a lifeboat crewman being put aboard the casualty to assist her home.

It happens from time to time – this time it was on 10 April 1983 when a holidaymaker found a red flare on the beach in the Port Appin area – and fired it! Before this information was received by the coastguard, the lifeboat was already off Port Appin and, of course, recalled. Time for really effective fines? The increased power and manoeuvrability of the Brede lead to many more services, which her predecessors could not have undertaken. There follows a selection of some of her "shouts".

A mayday call from a commercial fishing boat on 25 April 1983 resulted, as usual, in the gathering round her of several vessels answering the call. The casualty was aground on Lady Rock off Lismore Light with four persons aboard and so firmly aground in a strong, albeit flooding, tide that the attempt to tow her off was delayed until there was more water in order to avoid damage. After an hour, she came off gently and was escorted to Oban by the lifeboat. Once again it is worth noting that no RNLI coxswain would attempt to tow a grounded vessel off without first obtaining the master's agreement and acknowledgement that damage might occur. It is also only right to stress that neither would any coxswain adopt a "gung-ho", "let's get her off at any cost" attitude after getting the master's agreement.

During the annual lifeboat raft race in May, a single-handed Fisher 35 was seen entering the bay by the north channel but rather too near the Corran Ledge and was advised of this. The message was copied by the lifeboat, which, already on duty for the raft race, quickly landed a crewman on the Fisher to assist and found the sole sailor in a fairly weak state through loss of blood from a crushed finger. The HMA met the casualty at the South Pier and took the patient to hospital where he had eight stitches put in his hand.

This month also saw Coxswain Patrick Maclean selected to join the RNLI contingent, which attended the International Lifeboat Conference, that year in Gothenburg, Sweden, in a Brede-class lifeboat.

At 0103 on 14 June 1983 coastguard reported the 20-ft yacht *Wigeon* with two persons on board had broken from her mooring in Craignure Bay, Isle of Mull and, with her outboard engine failed, was being driven towards the steep-to shores of the Isle of Bernera and the nearby reef of Liath Sgeir. The night was overcast and the wind WNW Force 7 gusting 8. Under the command of Second Coxswain Douglas Craig the lifeboat was launched at 0110 and gained a fix by radio direction finder on the yacht whose occupants, a husband and wife, were, understandably, sounding somewhat distressed. The wind had backed more to the west and was over the new flood tide and the casualty advised she was rolling heavily. Ensuring that the "jury" sea anchor of warps had been recovered by the yacht, Second Coxswain Craig made a few runs alongside taking off the lady on one and her husband on another. Conditions were such that it was considered too dangerous to put a man aboard to secure a towline on the yacht and the lifeboat returned to Oban where conditions at the South Pier pontoon prevented the landing of the survivors. They were landed at the North Pier and taken to the boathouse before spending the night at the Royal National Mission to Deep Sea Fishermen, then a much used haven. The fishing boat *Lilacina* succeeded in securing a tow on the *Wigeon* and she was eventually moored at Ardentrive, Kerrera.

For this service, Second Coxswain Craig and his crew, Malcolm Robertson, Sydney Thomson and Willie Melville were recipients of a Letter of Appreciation signed by the then director of the RNLI, Rear Admiral Wilf Graham.

A search by several boats, including the lifeboat (which was recalled later) in July for an overdue small outboard dinghy in the Crinan area ended happily when she arrived under oars, having suffered engine failure. The occupant had been checking livestock on various small islands but reports that there were no lifejackets or flares on board caused some concern.

Two days later, 38 passengers and three crewmen on board an Oban pleasure boat would have made a very "chummy" gathering had it been necessary to evacuate them to the Brede following the grounding of their own craft on a rock west of Kerrera when looking at seals. After assessing the position,

Coxswain Maclean and the launch's skipper decided to attempt to tow her off and, within 25 minutes of grounding, with passengers still aboard, she was refloated, inspected for damage and escorted back to Oban. Once over their anxiety, the passengers appeared to enjoy the experience and, no doubt, would dine out on the story for some time.

On 26 July 1983 a German holidaymaker in an inflatable dinghy was reported missing in Loch Craignish and the lifeboat launched. When it was advised, a few minutes after the launch, that the missing man was a diabetic, she returned to pick up the HMA. Visibility was very poor and slow progress was made using both radar and a bow lookout. Once in the search area, auxiliary coastguard Nick Ryan's *Sgarbh,* also searching, reported seeing the casualty on the shore where the lifeboat found him and established that he had gone ashore overnight to await the lifting of the fog.

Later on the same day, a hovercraft with one skipper and nine passengers suffered engine failure at the mouth of Loch Feochan some 4 miles South of Oban, a sometimes difficult tidal area. With no commercial tow able to be arranged it was necessary to launch the lifeboat which was able to take the hovercraft in tow back to Oban. The tow was carried out at a very slow speed in order to avoid damage to the hovercraft's "skirt" which, as a result of the power failure, was trailing in the water.

The remaining services of the year were: (a) assistance to an overdue assault craft with six persons on board; (b) recalled from answering a mayday (reduced to a "Pan"); (c) a medivac from Mull; and (d) transfer of the HMA to the island of Kerrera to attend to a man crushed when the boat he was working at fell on him – sadly he did not survive.

The new year of 1984 was only two days old when the first medivac was carried out. The need to transfer the lady to hospital in Oban had been anticipated from New Year's Day and agreement reached that, if it were necessary, the transfer should be made at slack water. When the patient's health deteriorated and the forecast indicated further deterioration in the weather as well, the lifeboat launched at 0858 hours reaching Craignure linkspan at 0935 hours. The patient left the South Pier, Oban by ambulance to hospital at 1040 hours. At the time of writing, the RNLI's Sea Safety initiative (of which more later) appears to be highly successful, especially in the field of lifejacket awareness. Many lifejackets carry the words "useless unless worn" or words to that effect. They would do well to add the words "especially with crotch-straps". One sailor in the mouth of Loch Etive in June 1984 may well have survived had he had a crotch-strap fitted to his lifejacket. Without its restraining influence his lifejacket was allowed to ride up under his armpits leaving his head under water. Wind on the day at the scene was WxN Force 7/8 and the sea, even in relatively sheltered water, moderate to choppy while the dinghy, which had capsized throwing the two men (one survived) into the water, was only 6 ft 6 in long!

Engine failure due to dirty fuel can happen to any vessel but it becomes a bit embarrassing when it happens to a lifeboat – even when not on a service but merely on passage between stations. So it was, however, in June, when a lifeboat on passage and heading for Oban advised coastguard that she was experiencing fuel problems with BOTH (a good indicator) engines. Oban lifeboat duly met her and escorted her into Oban where the problem was put right.

A straightforward but nonetheless important service was carried out on 22 June 1984 when a 37-ton commercial fishing vessel, with four persons on board, had the misfortune to run aground in Gylen Bay, Kerrera. Using the fishing boat's own liferaft and a rocket-propelled speedline, all four were transferred to the Brede, the liferaft recovered and the fishing boat's crew taken to the Royal National Mission for Deep Sea Fishermen in Oban.

The message from the coastguard was "vessel unable to find Oban". The wind at the time was light north westerly, the weather fine and clear and it was 1500 hours on the 7 August 1984 – what was the problem? That the vessel was a chartered boat, perhaps not in the hands of very experienced people, may have explained the call. She had been on passage from Onich to Oban, a distance of some 20 miles or thereby. The

30

lifeboat, already at sea, was advised and, estimating that the casualty ought to be somewhere in the Lismore Light/Morvern area, began searching there. At 1542, however, the coastguard received a message from the vessel that she had just passed the Ardluing Buoy, south of the island of Luing – some 15 miles PAST Oban! Courses to Oban were given to her and the lifeboat resumed her work with a BBC film unit! The BBC programme being made was for Gaelic TV and entitled *A Cheud Turus* (*The First Time*). On board that day, along with presenter Angela MacEachern, were a few schoolboys who found the whole experience fascinating.

What might be described as a "juggling" act took place on the evening of 8 August when the Brede, already on service to a yacht stranded on the rocks in the Falls of Lora, under Connel Bridge and listing badly, received a second call to search for a dinghy with two persons aboard which was adrift from the Yeoman Quarry at Glensanda on the Ardgour shore. When it was established that the original casualty would not refloat until around 0130 the following morning, a crew member was put aboard to assist in preparing for the attempt and to establish communications, the yacht being unable to transmit. Now short-handed, the lifeboat took aboard one of her crew members not involved but watching events from the bridge above and set out to search the Lynn of Morvern for the dinghy. Fortunately this second service was not a long one, the dinghy and occupants turning up safely, allowing *Ann Ritchie* to return her attention to the grounded yacht. The three persons aboard were transferred to the lifeboat at 2314 hours and were returned to their yacht when she refloated at 0120 hours whereupon they accepted the coxswain's offer to escort them to an anchorage inside the loch where he advised that they remain until slack high water until they could proceed seawards later that morning.

Not many services by lifeboats to vessels aground result in the rock/s they are stranded upon being "named" – even unofficially. However, a nasty piece of "real estate", a rock just north of Innis, off Easdale is now referred to by Oban Lifeboat crew as "the Northumbria Rose rock". It has caught out a few experienced navigators (as we shall see later) but one of the strandings which took up some 22 hours of the lifeboat's time occurred on 19 August 1984 when the coaster *Northumbria Rose* with a crew of six, bound Runcorn from Lochaline in patches of fog, failed to avoid it. The *Ann Ritchie* launched at 0205 hours and, on arrival, found that the casualty, although listing to starboard, was in no immediate danger and stood by her until high water expected at 1041 hours. Several attempts at this time, assisted by the cargo vessel *Aberthaw Fisher* resulted in tow lines parting, including the *Aberthaw Fisher*'s insurance wire and the decision to await a further high water was taken. Apart from the coxswain, a fresh lifeboat crew was arranged and divers inspected the casualty finding that she was mainly held some 25 ft from her bow. The shout-within-a-shout habit seemed to be "catching" when coastguard reported the discharge of a smoke float seen in the Garvellochs area and the lifeboat, still only standing by the casualty, left to investigate but, despite landing a man on the island, found nothing. The Brede returned to the *Northumbria Rose* at 2037 hours but further attempts to tow her off were abandoned at 2320 hours. The *Ann Ritchie* was home, refuelled and ready for service at 0040 hours on 20 August 1984.

The assessment of a service on 30 August read "saved boat and gave assistance". A 3-ton fishing boat (two persons aboard) with engine failure anchored near the north end of the island of Shuna, Appin, was dragging anchor and required assistance. When the lifeboat arrived on scene the casualty was approximately 100 yds off the shore. Lines were passed and assistance given to recover her anchors before she was towed to nearby Dallens Bay before her crew were taken aboard the lifeboat and taken back to Oban.

A service on 2 September had the hon sec scratching his head only when it came to recording the cause of the medical evacuation from Mull – *shocked haematemesis* – fortunately for the crew, Gordon Murchison, HMA, was one of them that night.

Of the three services carried out on 9 September 1984, the most unusual was the first – unusual in that the coxswain was in charge but not aboard – in fact, the lifeboat never left her moorings.   At about 0330 in a westerly wind Force 8, occasionally 9, heavy rain squalls and a rough sea, six vessels moored on the South Pier pontoons were finding their position untenable, one of them having already suffered considerable damage.   Coxswain Maclean and Hon Sec MacLeod considered that, rather than launching the lifeboat to assist perhaps one boat at a time, it was more expedient to use all of the lifeboat crew in letting go all of the vessels putting one crewmember aboard each and assisting her to the shelter of Ardentrive Bay, Kerrera.   Six lifeboat crewmembers under the supervision of the coxswain did just this while Second Coxswain Craig, in the yard boat *Dirk,* directed the boats to appropriate moorings.   By 0630 all were secured and the lifeboat crew returned to the station.

The two remaining calls that day were fairly routine, the first being a capsized sailing dinghy from which the lifeboat was recalled and the second, the evacuation from a yacht to Oban hospital of a man with severe head injuries.

On the evening of 28 September 1984, two or more reports of white and green flares were reported between the islands of Kerrera and Mull. The lifeboat was launched but found nothing on her first run from Maiden Island to the William Black Memorial Tower on the Mull shore.   The first informant, a yacht, confirmed that her first sighting had been in the region of Bach Island ("Pot Lid") while the lifeboat reported an occasional weak flash a few cables to the north of the south tip of Kerrera. All this appeared strange and while coastguard had some reports of meteor activity in the area there is still some opinion that these lights were connected in some way with drug-running which came to the surface not so long afterwards.

A 110-ft Danish fishing vessel with an injured seaman aboard called the coastguard at 1954 hours on 21 October for both medical and navigational assistance – the latter probably because she would originally have had no intention to close the shore and, therefore, would not carry such charts. The HMA decided to treat the man on arrival in Oban and the lifeboat proceeded to the casualty's position just south of the Torran Rocks. Good radio and radar contact was made and the fishing vessel was advised to follow the lifeboat 1 mile astern and that a lifeboat crewman would be put aboard prior to entering Oban Bay. Second Coxswain Douglas Craig was landed on the casualty 2 miles south west of Maiden Island and the injured seaman transferred to hospital when the vessel berthed at the North Pier.

One of the services that will always remain memorable in station records took place on 31 January 1985. The 80-ton (net) fishing vessel *Shemara* had gone aground on Lady Rock off the south end of the island of Lismore, with eight persons on board in a WNW wind of Force 7/8. The *Ann Ritchie* launched at 0332 and, on arrival at the Rock, found the vessel listing 30-40 degrees to port. The five crewmen who had taken to a liferaft were back aboard, the liferaft itself, having been in danger of going on the rocks.

The casualty's skipper reported there was about a fathom of water on his <u>starboard</u> side and suggested it would be enough for the lifeboat. After considering the position, Coxswain Pat Maclean opted to try to take the crew off from the <u>port</u> quarter of the casualty. Although there was more water there, the casualty's port list, the strong wind and the seas from astern, the presence of rocks all around and the backwash from the rocks ahead all made the job an extremely difficult one.

Coxswain Maclean made around 14 approaches in all – some abortive – but, by 0405 hours, all eight fishing boat crewmembers had been safely taken aboard the lifeboat, the casualty's skipper suffering angina pains. A high degree of seamanship and boathandling was demonstrated by the coxswain in this service and the remaining crew on the foredeck did what was required in exemplary fashion.

It should be recognised that, by going against the skipper's suggestion the coxswain was "putting his head on the block" had the outcome gone against him. In the event, the only damage sustained by the lifeboat was a small chip on the toerail of the starboard shoulder.

Not surprisingly, the RNLI recognised the success and the excellence of this service by awarding the thanks of the Institution on vellum together with a Service of Merit badge to Coxswain Patrick Maclean and vellum Service Certificates to crewmembers Billy Forteith, David Graham and Mike Robertson.

The story was picked up by "Silk Cut" who entered it in the bravery category of their annual nautical awards. The station was extremely proud when the news reached Oban that Pat and his crew that night had been awarded first place and presented with the Silk Cut gold medal.

Services to vessels of 500 tons do not occur very often but the Brede's first was to assist the commercial survey ship *Sea Trans Surveyor* aground on the Ferry Rocks in the Sound of Kerrera just 1.5 miles from the station. Twenty-two persons were aboard and the lifeboat's first task was to take ten "non-essential" personnel off, landing them at the South Pier. The casualty reported no damage to her tanks and was pumping out her ballast. Having sounded around the casualty's stern the lifeboat passed a tow-line, re-floated her and escorted her to Oban North Pier.

Just why a fishing boat would want to discharge two rounds from a shotgun on 7 August 1985 is anybody's guess – that is, however, exactly what happened! Reports ranging from "two loud bangs" to "flashes with shape" were received and the lifeboat was launched to investigate. One vessel on the line of the sightings did report that she had discharged two shots about the time in question and repeated the firing by way of demonstration. All agreed that this was what had been originally heard, that there was no vessel in difficulty and the *Ann Ritchie* returned to station.

Another "first" – a call-out in the middle of the soup course at the annual crew dinner on 22 December 1985. Despite the timing, the entire crew present rushed to be able to grab one of the four places available. No one was driving on that evening and, out on George Street, a poor motorist had his car commandeered to take the crew to the station. It transpired that he was a lifeboat supporter, one Neil MacAulay and had always wanted to "do something like this"! The unsuccessful candidates returned to the hotel to have dinner and the odd libation while awaiting the return of the crew. The shout was in answer to flares reported between the Isle of Colonsay and the Garvellochs but, after 2/3 hours searching, nothing was found and the lucky (?) four returned to the party about 1.30am.

Medical evacuations to Oban hospital are mainly from the Isle of Mull and, true to form, the first of the new year on 7 February was a suspected appendicitis case from Fionnphort but the next on the following day was to attend to a fisherman aboard a French boat shooting creels south of the Garvellochs. The man had accidentally stepped into a bight of the rope snaking fast through a fairlead at which he was brought up short, breaking a leg and losing the tip of a finger. Dr Murchison and a lifeboat crewmember were put aboard the fishing vessel and the compound fracture was reduced using an inflatable splint while the hand was dressed and an IV fluids line set up before the patient was taken aboard the lifeboat for transfer to hospital in Oban. The HMA's request to his colleague to search for the fingertip on the deck was obeyed but fruitless.

Not all accidents that a lifeboat requires to attend in this area of the Highlands occur at sea. On 17 March 1986, during the installation of a new power line to the quarry at Glensanda on the remote Morvern peninsula, a tracked vehicle carrying six men overturned and plunged down the steep mountainside resulting in one fatality, three seriously injured men and two less seriously injured. With no road to the area, all rescue facilities had to be by sea and air – Oban lifeboat and an RAF helicopter from Leuchars were tasked, the lifeboat taking with her Dr Bruce Lennox, a good friend of the station who had been on several "shouts" with the crew.

The two casualties with less serious injuries were taken aboard the lifeboat while the helicopter transferred one of the remaining three to hospital in Oban returning to pick up the other two, one with spinal injuries and the other with serious head and facial damage both of whom were flown straight to hospital in Glasgow. During all of these activities two lifeboat crewmembers went ashore with a stretcher to assist in the transfer of the injured and in the co-ordination of the rescue. Later in the month a meeting of all concerned parties took place to discuss the event and assess what improvement in communications (if any) might be made should any similar emergency occur again.

It was fortunate for the two-man crew of a 26-ft creel boat off Loch Don in Mull on 18 March 1986 that their faint mayday message was picked up by the vessel *Lady Margaret* in the area with divers down. The creel boat had been holed and in imminent danger of sinking, one man in the water and the other on rocks, both being picked up by the divers' boat just as the creel boat sank. Both were transferred to the lifeboat, one of them hypothermic, and were taken at speed to the waiting ambulance at Oban.

A number of "personalities" visit the lifeboat from time to time but, on 22 May 1986, the lifeboat had to visit one of them. The powered pleasure craft *TV Big Softie* is likely to hint at the personality – he was, of course, Andy Robbins whose pet bear "Big Softie" appeared with him on television at that time. Having suffered engine failure in the tideway at Lismore Light, the Cal Mac ferry *Caledonia* stood by until the lifeboat arrived and took the casualty in tow to Gallanach.

On 15 June the lifeboat's Decca Navigator was a particularly useful "tool" in maintaining the search pattern when looking for a missing member of the crew of two of a small fishing vessel, which had capsized and sunk while lifting creels off Rubha nam Brathairean, Ross of Mull. In co-operation with a Wessex helicopter (remember them?) an area from close inshore to 5.5 cables off was systematically searched while a coast rescue team combed the shoreline. A few hours later the search had, sadly, to be terminated with the finding of a body by a diver close to the sunken boat.

On a completely different tack, the lifeboat's service on 20 July 1986 need never have been necessary. A woman with a young child in a small boat were reported by the Cal Mac ferry *Caledonia* to be in difficulty on the Corran Ledge, Oban Bay and the lifeboat was launched to investigate. On arrival, one crewmember rowed over to the "casualty" to discover that the shaft of the outboard had fouled the sewer pipe and would have been cleared if the lady had only known to tip the outboard upwards!

At 0253 hours on 1 August 1986, the lifeboat left her mooring in answer to a CB message received by the coastguard from a 20-ft motor-cruiser with no VHF radio.

A 20-ft Colvic motor-cruiser with four persons aboard was dragging anchor off the Alginate Factory, Loch Creran in south-easterly Force 6 wind. On arrival alongside the dragging boat one lifeboat crewman was put aboard and shocked to find that the four persons comprised three adults and a baby! All were safely taken to Yeoman's Rhugarbh Depot and the Colvic tied astern of the workboat *Lady Fiona*.

Anxiety as to the whereabouts of the owner of a yacht, which was found high and dry on a rock between Creagan Inn and the old railway bridge in Loch Creran, led to the launch of the boat at 0135 hours on 13 August. The owner had been resident in Creagan Inn but had failed to show up that night. On reaching the scene at 0254 hours the lifeboat heard a radio on board the casualty but nobody to be seen. In view of the difficulty of approach and the strong tide flowing through the narrows, Crewmember David Graham, in a dry-suit and with a rope paid out from the lifeboat around him, swam ashore to investigate. As he quietly bent over the recumbent form in the boat, trying to establish whether it was dead or alive, the "body" awoke with a roar and whether David or the owner was the nearer to a heart attack at that point is a matter of conjecture. With neither the boat nor the owner in immediate danger, the lifeboat headed for home – WITH David!

On 14 November 1986 the creel boat *Alicia* with two persons aboard broadcast a mayday message advising that she was making water fast and in danger of sinking just off the Ross of Mull. Several other fishing boats, a Northern Lighthouse Board helicopter and a Sea King helicopter were in the area and all aware of the emergency. The lifeboat was launched at 1350 hours but, before any of these could reach the scene, *Alicia* sank, the two crewmembers inflating their dinghy and paddling ashore safely. They were not, however, in such a state of panic that they left their catch behind to be returned to the sea – oh no! – their lobsters joined them in the dinghy and all were brought back to Oban in the lifeboat. The lifeboat crew were also the beneficiaries, each receiving a fresh lobster – no more than one would expect of owner/skipper, Graham Clark, one of life's gentlemen. The world is a poorer place for his sad passing on 7 August 2006.

The then hon sec at Oban, Captain Norman MacLeod, is never a man to "cry wolf" or make requests without lengthy consideration of what his coxswain told him. After an unnecessarily difficult service in dense fog on 28 April 1987 because of the lack of a quarter mile range on the radar, he did make an earnest plea for the fitting of a new radar with just such a range.

Craignure Bay, Mull in a north-westerly force 6/7, dragging anchor and a fouled propeller – not what the five persons aboard a charter yacht on 2 May 1987 would have chosen but it's what they had! A mayday was broadcast and the lifeboat launched at 2235 hours reaching the casualty at 2312 to find that she had stopped dragging and had managed to secure to a mooring. The mayday was cancelled, all five persons were taken aboard the lifeboat and transferred to the Royal National Mission for Deep Sea Fishermen in Oban.

One of the occasional "double" services took place on 24 May 1987 when a yacht was reported aground off Ardsheal, Duror. The lifeboat was launched at 2256 hours and, during her passage to Duror was advised to look out for the yacht *Mahla* overdue in Oban. Reports of northerly winds 4-5 seemed overstated until the lifeboat left the fairly calm waters inside Lismore and found the wind/sea just as reported. The yacht, *Zeta* was located with both bower and kedge anchors streamed but still bumping in the moderate sea although expected to re-float fully in about 20 minutes on the rising tide. At that time the lifeboat was directed to search Port na Morlachd, Lismore and then the west side of the island for the missing *Mahla* during which the *Zeta* was reported as re-floated and proceeding to Ballachulish. About the same time *Mahla* was stated to now be safely on her mooring at Oban. The lifeboat returned to station and was ready for service again by 0500 hours. Once more, radar with a range of a quarter mile would have been invaluable for searching areas with limited manoeuvring space.

When the Contessa 26 *Maid of Aros* caught fire in Salen Bay, Mull on 27 May 1987 the lifeboat was launched only to be recalled at Lismore Light, not only because the yacht *Amidas* was coping but because the owner, the late Captain David Mellis, then 72 years old, had swum ashore!

Occasionally when an immediate launch is necessary within a stone's throw of the station, it is justifiable to launch without the full complement of crew. Such was the position on 27 May 1987 when the Oban Sailing Club's rescue boat "shed" her helmsman when a sponson collapsed under him. The first informant, George Seaton, then commodore of Oban Sailing Club, joined Coxswain Pat Maclean and Crewmember David Graham on the lifeboat and set about recovering the empty rescue boat which was going round in circles, her helmsman having been picked up by a fish farm launch. After several attempts to secure her, she was eventually brought to a stop by floating a line into her propeller.

The launching authority's remarks on the return of service in respect of one "shout" in July 1987 says it all – "a thoroughly incompetent crew on the casualty made the coxswain's task almost impossible". At 0214 hours the lifeboat launched in search of a 39-ft MFV-type vessel overdue in Oban and found her not far from home with engine failure. A towline was set up and course was made for the North Pier, Oban when the casualty mysteriously regained power, went ahead and overtook the lifeboat. The tow was immediately cast off, the MFV's engine stopped and she was lashed alongside the lifeboat only to re-start her engine and, this time, go full astern. Again the tow was dropped and she was directed to the North Pier running aground three times on the way! Once there, the second coxswain was put aboard and berthed the casualty without further excitement.

Remarkable progress has been made in Search and Rescue techniques over the last 20 years or so, not the least of which has been in field of signalling danger or difficulty. One of the most advanced pieces of safety equipment is the EPIRB (emergency position indicating radio beacon). Signals from such beacons are picked up by Search and Rescue satellites (SARSAT), which transmit the position of the signal with incredible accuracy to the appropriate rescue services. Sailors in distress welcome such sophisticated equipment although the "downside" can be highly embarrassing for the hapless individual who accidentally activates an EPIRB perhaps when laying up the boat for the winter. Oban Lifeboat has on more than one occasion been called to search for such a signal using direction finding equipment one of the first being on 10 August 1987 when SARSAT reported an EPIRB "hit" between Loch Spelve and Loch Creran. Shortly after launching, the lifeboat's direction finder indicated that the source was really very close and after 9 minutes identified it as being a yacht in Ardentrive Bay, Oban in process of being laid up for the winter.

The Caledonian Canal is regularly used, especially by fishing boats, to switch from east to west coasts and *vice versa*. Such was the purpose of the 55-ft trawler *Early Dawn* on 27 October 1987 heading from Cumbria to Corpach to enter the canal. At 2217 she ran aground on the unlit Branra Rock 7.5 miles NxE of the station. With the vessel listing dangerously about 35/40 degrees and her starboard rail under water, the four crew had taken to the liferaft. Discussion between skipper and lifeboat coxswain resulted in the skipper authorising the lifeboat to try to tow the casualty off. At this point the water level was 9 in from the wheelhouse door so there was little time to spare. After numerous attempts, *Early Dawn* re-floated at 2342 showing no signs of taking water and was escorted to Oban by the lifeboat. This was an excellent service for there is little doubt that, had Coxswain Maclean not made every effort to tow the trawler off, she would probably have filled and gone down.

At least one of the party of eight divers off Heather Island in the Sound of Kerrera must have had at least Boy Scout knowledge of Morse Code when their boat suffered power failure on 15 November. They had no VHF radio but, using a torch, signalled "SOS" and were fortunate that one person who saw it could read Morse! The lifeboat took all eight persons aboard and towed the disabled boat back to the South Pier – job completed and lifeboat refuelled and ready for service again 44 minutes after the first report.

That a 25-ft fishing vessel was able to be towed into Oban by the lifeboat one evening a fortnight before Christmas 1987 is down to the vigilance of a nearby trawler *Early Dawn*. The casualty had suffered mechanical failure but, with neither radio nor flares on board, resorted to the flashing of her working lights. This signal, fortunately, was seen by the crew of the *Early Dawn* who called the coastguard and the lifeboat was launched. This tortuous method of signalling falls into the category of "avoidable" and it is highly likely that this casualty now carries both radio and flares.

Even amongst the many, many routine services which were carried out by the Brede – from medical evacuations to the finding and towing home of missing and overdue vessels to the countless services from which she was recalled before reaching the scene, some remain vivid in the memory perhaps because of some simple happening during the "shout". All of the crew on a service in Loch Etive on Good Friday 1988 (searching for a possible canoeist who turned out not to be missing at all) will probably still remember the ingenuity of the mechanic that day, the late Malcolm Robertson. Up at Kinlochetive, Malcolm, feeling like his first cigarette of the afternoon, discovered that there were no matches aboard, no other crewman smoked and therefore no means of ignition was available. The resourceful Malcolm unscrewed the magnifying glass from the radar set and, under a hot sun, set fire to a paper "taper"!

Fire at sea is one of the dangers which seamen fear most. Fortunately, on 16 April 1988, the vessel on fire, the FV *Kerloch,* was alongside the North Pier, Oban and the second out from the pier, the inside berth being occupied by the FV *Pen Glas.* At six minutes after midnight, the lifeboat found her with deck and wheelhouse burning fiercely. Firemen were already aboard and Second Coxswain Douglas Craig boarded the *Kerloch* and shut down her engine while lifeboat HMA Gordon Murchison also went aboard to attend to the only remaining crewmember who was taken by the lifeboat to the pier steps and thence by ambulance to hospital. The fire extinguished, the lifeboat then towed the casualty clear of the *Pen Glas* to a fresh berth and returned to station, ready for service again at 0145. Throughout this service there was a danger that any gas cylinders aboard might explode.

The loss of life as a result of falling overboard is always a sad occurrence but the circumstances in which the individual lost his life in Loch Melfort on 17 July 1988 was particularly so. The yacht *Heisgeir* returning to Loch Melfort from a cruise on the west coast with two families aboard had all but completed the passage and was passing Kames Bay, approaching the moorings when one male fell overboard or was knocked over by the swinging boom. It appears that, being so nearly home, he had removed his lifejacket, which he had worn constantly throughout the cruise. This habit of casting off the lifejacket when reaching "home waters" is not uncommon amongst sailors – writer included. Reports from the yacht indicated that, for a few moments, his boots were seen on the surface then quickly disappeared. The lifeboat launched at 1645 and was requested by HMCG to assume the role of "on scene commander", there being approximately 30 craft searching. She asked that the yacht *Drum* continue as OSC until her arrival. On reaching the loch she took over and initially instructed the "fleet" to continue their present sweep. To complicate matters, a crewmember of *Drum* fell from the mast (from where he, doubtless, had been scanning the water) sustaining a broken leg. The lifeboat organised an ambulance, a doctor from another yacht and evacuated the injured man to an ambulance. She laid a mark at the "man overboard" position and continued searching until 2030 when, in consultation with coastguard, the search was called off, the helicopter stood down and the pan pan broadcast cancelled. She then escorted *Heisgeir* to her mooring, and landed the crew. She was ready for service in Oban again just before midnight.

At 0314 hours on 25 July 1988 the lifeboat (the relief boat *Merchant Navy*) answered a call from a motor yacht dragging her anchor in Cuan Sound in south south-east winds of Force 7 and above, the two persons aboard being a husband and wife the former having collapsed attempting to lay a second anchor. An ambulance and doctor left Oban by road for Cuan Ferry from where the lifeboat landed the doctor on board the motor yacht where he pronounced the husband dead. The local ferrymen were extremely kind and helpful, taking care of both the lady and the boat. The lifeboat returned to Oban at 0500 and was ready for service again at 0530 hours.

Before 10am that same morning however, she was launched on what turned out to be a "multi-service" lasting a further five hours. Records show that the winds at times during the five hours involved were south south-west 7-8 occasionally 9-11 (well in excess of 60 knots) and the sea state "very rough" with a swell of 20-25 ft. Extracts from that day's records will perhaps convey a flavour of the service:

"1015 HMCG report two boys missing on the island of Kerrera. Lifeboat requested to convey police and coastguard to the island. Done.

1100 Lifeboat requested to divert to Puilladobhrain to recover four persons from a motor yacht who are marooned on an islet.

Lifeboat to assist a yacht in trouble in Loch Spelve, her anchor cable having parted.

Under way for Loch Spelve, lifeboat sights another yacht lost and on wrong course in heavy seas. Lifeboat escorts her to the entrance of the Sound of Kerrera and resumes course for Loch Spelve.

Lifeboat ships spare anchor from another yacht and puts aboard the original drifting casualty.

Lifeboat responds to mayday call from boat in Puilladobhrainn.

Under way to the mayday casualty. HMCG advise situation there resolved but requests lifeboat to return to Oban Bay to assist yacht in distress there.

1330 In Oban Bay – find the yacht aground on Corran Ledge – no-one aboard.

Tow her off and place her on mooring at Ardentrive.

Refuelled and ready for service."

A busy five hours! Conditions like these not expected in the month of July.

It is heartening to realise that we are all looked after by our fellow men and women more than we realise. On 29 August a member of the public saw what he/she thought was a swimmer/surfer in difficulties off Ganavan and phoned the coastguard who requested immediate launch of the lifeboat. Arriving on scene 12 minutes after the pagers the lifeboat was pleased to hear from another surfer that his buddy was diving off his board from time to time to take underwater photographs!

Before the re-introduction of a lifeboat to Tobermory in 1990 most of the Sound of Mull fell into Oban Lifeboat's "patch" and calls were not unknown as far up as Ardmore Point (see ILB service on 11 September 1974 for example). On 4 October 1988 a 50-ft fishing vessel ran aground near the Glenmorvern Boathouse and began taking water with which her pumps could not cope. Oban lifeboat was launched and, arriving on scene, found the casualty listing 50 degrees with her four crewmembers all on the high side of the hull. They were transferred, two at a time, by the lifeboat's X-boat and taken back to Oban where they were looked after by the Royal National Mission for Deep Sea Fishermen.

A medical evacuation from the island of Kerrera on 5 October 1988 of a patient with a severe asthma attack, requested by Dr Bruce Lennox, was concluded successfully when the patient was taken by ambulance from the Cal Mac linkspan to hospital. It is worth recording, however, that Dr Lennox was of the opinion that his patient's life had been saved by a combination of the prompt reaction of the lifeboat and the portable oxygen cylinder carried on board. This is also an appropriate juncture at which to say that Dr Lennox's premature retirement, through ill health, was a huge loss, not only to Oban Lifeboat to whom he was a great friend, but also to the community of Oban.

CHAPTER IV

1989-1993

The Brede Years (ii)

Most injuries to lifeboatmen usually occur at sea or on board – unlike those suffered by the Oban crew in February 1989. A farmer on the island of Kerrera had suffered a heart attack and required to be transferred to hospital in Oban – this at the request of his GP, Dr Kate Armstrong who accompanied the crew on board. For stretcher-handling purposes, one extra crewmember was carried as well. Despite sleet and hail squalls and a southerly wind of Force 6 gusting 7, the shore party of three crewmembers and the doctor was landed at the ferry slip where a tractor and trailer awaited to transport the four plus stretcher to the farmhouse, some half-mile away. Coxswain and one crewmember remained aboard.

Shortly afterwards a call was received from the shore party to advise that the trailer had capsized, two crew were injured and that the fourth crewmember was required ashore. This was done and the lifeboat moved south to stand off the beach as near to the farmhouse as possible and illuminate the route the stretcher party would now have to take. The patient was duly transferred to the lifeboat with stretcher athwartships on the small inflatable dinghy and taken by ambulance from the North Pier.

One crewmember, "Murch", was found to have a dislocated finger and Dr Kate, a cut scalp, but another, mechanic Jim Watson, did not fare so well – he suffered a broken shoulder socket which put him out of action for about six months.

Around now, the new South Pier workings were becoming increasingly inconvenient, even dangerous, for the lifeboat's activities. On 12 February 1989 when landing a stretcher-bound patient from Mull to the ambulance, the boat had to come in stern first to achieve a level between deck and slipway. In anything but calm weather this would have been impossible and highlighted the thoroughly unsatisfactory conditions under which the station was being required to work. A fear that the development of the whole South Pier area might lead to loss of the station altogether, drove the volunteer crew to action – this by way of a press release which came to be known locally as "The Mutiny". So important was the impact of this action, the full story is told in the next few paragraphs.

To describe the actions of a volunteer lifeboat crew as "mutiny" seems totally incongruous – but it came perilously close to the truth in January 1989. For the previous year, and more, development of the South Pier by the Scottish Development Agency (SDA) had been going on. To allow work to proceed, the lifeboat's mooring had been moved north-westerly into deeper water but any other effect of the work upon the lifeboat's activities had been totally ignored by the SDA. The installation of sheet-piling on the site of the former "beach" meant that the lifeboat crew in their boarding dinghy, if blown past the lifeboat when trying to launch to a call, would have no "way out" – a potentially highly dangerous situation.

The only practical site for a lifeboat mooring in Oban Bay, as any sea-wise person will agree, is in the South Pier area. To make it possible for the lifeboat to be retained here was obviously a very expensive business and, in the early stages, the SDA told all parties that they would take care of the re-location. The news that they were thought to be prepared to offer the derisory sum of £50,000 towards it came as a bolt from the blue.

"Enough is enough" the crew thought and issued a press release on 9 January 1989. This statement was issued by the volunteer crew only – they being anxious not to compromise the positions of the full-time coxswain/mechanic or the headquarters-appointed honorary secretary. In particular, their statement that "this crew will not vacate their existing lifeboat station until proper provision has been made for permanent replacement" aroused the interest of the Press to such an extent that both local and national papers took up the cause. The SDA spokesman who said "OK – so you have to tread on a few toes along the way – but it (*the new pier*) means a big fillip for Oban at large" probably now regrets his statement.

The press release clearly touched a raw nerve somewhere in the SDA who quickly invited RNLI representatives to a meeting three days later! The outcome, greatly assisted by the late Sir Charles McGrigor, former convenor of the Scottish Lifeboat Council, was an agreement that a new berth for the lifeboat would be constructed in the area of the Port Beag slip, with lion's share of the cost being met by the SDA, although the RNLI contributed a not inconsiderable sum. The "icing on the cake", as it were, for the Institution was the 99-year lease by Argyll and Bute Council of the vacant 180-year-old listed building South Pier House at a "peppercorn" rent of £1 per annum. The crew, using a substantial sum from their own funds, made initial improvements and later the Institution re-designed the interior entirely. The trim, white-washed, cottage-like building with twin turrets now comprises office, gear-store, sitting room, shower room and fundraising store. A satisfactory ending but only after a struggle, which a prominent charity like the RNLI ought never to have had.

Although, as said earlier, the hon sec, Norman MacLeod, had been excluded by the crew from their protest, he was totally behind them. When, during one of the meetings to thresh out the problem, it was put to him by the SDA that he really must not allow his men to negotiate through the Press (*or words to that effect*), his eloquent reply left everyone in no doubt whatsoever that their action had his full backing and would continue to have it under the circumstances.

Access to the huge quarry at Glensanda on the Morvern peninsula is mainly by sea and when a serious fire was reported there on 13 May 1989 the lifeboat was, not surprisingly, requested to convey the firemaster and brigade personnel from Oban. Other teams of firemen were being transported from Port Appin and Rhugarbh by the quarry's own launches. Having established that no one was missing and no injured personnel required to be taken to hospital in Oban, the lifeboat returned to station and was ready for service again at 0046 hours on 14 May.

On 10 June it was the turn of the police authorities to request assistance from Oban Lifeboat to convey two constables to the island of Colonsay where an individual had assaulted not only a pregnant lady but also the special constable who had tried to apprehend him. Although Colonsay is within Islay Lifeboat area, there were no available extra constables on Islay and the task had to be undertaken by Oban Police. The lifeboat arrived at Colonsay at 2325 hours leaving again at 0105 hours with police and the offender aboard.

Some terrain in the Oban Lifeboat area is such that the recovery of injured persons has sometimes to be by a fairly circuitous route. And so it was on 2 July 1989 when a man fell from cliffs one mile north of Easdale and the lifeboat attended. Two crewmembers were landed to find a doctor and ambulancemen with the casualty. One crewmember rowed the casualty and the doctor out to the lifeboat lying off which took them to Easdale from where the HMA's car transferred the patient to hospital in Oban. The lifeboat returned to the scene to evacuate the ambulancemen and recover the remaining crewmember.

The remaining months of 1989 saw a mixture of routine calls – the transfer of an "overdose" patient from Mull to Oban, an abortive launch to an inebriated man who was attempting to swim Loch Leven at Ballachulish instead of walking over the bridge, various strandings and the usual medivacs and "pregivacs". One of the last of the year was to "push" a fishing boat on fire, alongside the pier where the fire brigade brought the blaze under control.

Nineteen-ninety started with the usual variety of evacuations from the Isle of Mull, the first being a "double" – one heart attack and one pregnancy on the same "shout" – followed by a search for overdue canoeists (found safe) and overdue divers (surfaced away from mother boat and found safe on the shore). In March an assault craft with 11 divers on board capsized off Eiln Mor, Dunstaffnage Bay and although all were picked up, one was unconscious and, despite the use of the lifeboat's ambu bag and a defibrillator from the ambulance, this one diver could not be resuscitated.

Lifeboats afloat are never "off duty". Oban lifeboat, returning to base after re-fit on the Clyde in June 1990, encountered a sailing dinghy with four persons aboard in Loch Fyne. She had been dismasted and the wind was northwesterly Force 5 so three of her crew were taken aboard the lifeboat and the fourth remained aboard to steer as the lifeboat made the slow passage to Tarbert – there the tow was slipped and the crew landed – all in a day's work !

On 2 June 1990 a medivac from Mull was to bring over a patient who had severed a "big toe" with a Flymo – records do not show whether or not the big toe accompanied him.

If the first informant's knowledge of Morse had been better, the launch at 20 minutes past midnight on 10 July need not have taken place. What the report said was (sic) "a yacht in Carsaig Bay is flashing what looks like SOS". What, in fact, he was seeing was the yacht owner checking his anchor or mooring by torchlight.

The need for a dedicated lifeboat slip was again highlighted on 6 August when the only means of landing an injured lady from the sail training vessel Sea Spirit was found to be by using the Cal Mac linkspan – fortunately the linkspan operator was on hand to lower it to the appropriate height and the incoming ferry from the Isle of Colonsay stood off until the transfer to the ambulance was completed.

Fresh WSW winds veering to WNW on 18-19 September 1990 resulted in the lifeboat attending to four vessels in two services. On the 18th she was launched to assist a 65-ft sailing ketch dragging anchor in Ardentrive Bay, Isle of Kerrera in winds of between 6 and 8 and with only one person aboard. In view of there being only one person on the casualty and the strength of the wind, two additional crewmembers were embarked on the lifeboat. Three lifeboat crew were put aboard the ketch to assist in the difficult job of recovering and clearing the fouled chain, using only a hand-cranked windlass. They also had to confirm that the fishing vessel to which the casualty had attached herself as a last resort, was still secure – they, in fact, landed two of the fishing vessel's own crew on their boat and assisted in attaching an additional strop to her mooring. Meantime, a yacht moored nearby sought lifeboat advice as she was being bumped by the concrete pontoon. She was advised to tie up to the pontoon and was kept under supervision from the lifeboat. The fishing vessel's two crewmembers were recovered to the lifeboat and the original casualty left lying to her own anchor once more – all 70 fathoms of her chain veered. Lifeboat ready for service again at 2300 hours.

At 1002 next morning the same 65-ft ketch advised she was again adrift in a rough sea and requiring assistance. Again three lifeboat crewmembers were put aboard her (there still being only one person aboard) and, with great effort weighed the anchor with its 70 fathoms of chain and attached wire and rubbish! The casualty was then escorted to a mooring at Heather Island assisted further by a lifeboat crewmember attaching an extra warp to the mooring buoy. On her way back to the station she received a request from a fishing boat alongside the Railway Pier to assist a neighbouring boat, suffering damage from the rough sea running. The lifeboat pulled the problem boat ahead and secured her before landing three of the lifeboat crew at the South Pier, the three remaining men still aboard on the mooring awaiting a lull to be able to come ashore in the dinghy. After about an hour they were able to do so.

For the part he played in the two services to the ketch, lifeboat Crewmember David Graham was given a special mention. Apart from expending much physical effort, he was in virtual command of the operation aboard the casualty where he made sensible decisions and communicated clearly with both Lifeboat and those on board the ketch.

Boarding Oban lifeboat on her mooring in the south-east corner of the bay in fresh north-westerly winds was never easy and so it was on the evening of 20 September 1990 when, in a WNW wind, Force 7-9, it was considered prudent to have a crew on stand-by aboard in readiness for slipping. A 31-ft yacht, with six persons aboard, was adrift off Loch Aline in the Sound of Mull. Tobermory Lifeboat was proceeding and the FV *Kyle Rona* was reported to be ten minutes away from the casualty. She was reported to be making about 5 knots over the ground and well within our "patch" – hence the "stand-by". In the event *Kyle Rona* took her under tow and returned to Loch Aline, escorted by Tobermory Lifeboat. The effort made and the potential danger to crew in embarking and disembarking in these conditions yet again showed how much the proposed new berth is required in Oban.

A "go-stop-go" service commenced at 3am on 14 October when the lifeboat with doctor and midwife on board, left to pick up a pregnant lady from Mull. Two minutes later, however, she was recalled, the baby having arrived. Three and a half hours later, complications with the baby's mother's health demanded that she be urgently hospitalised in Oban and the same coxswain, doctor and midwife, with two fresh crewmembers, landed mother and baby at Oban at 8.20 am.

An unusual service took place on 18 November 1990 when HM Customs requested assistance to disembark 12 persons from the warship HMS *Glasgow,* the weather conditions of NW winds of Force 7/8 not being suitable for small-boat transfer. Once alongside the *Glasgow*, five customs officers and seven prisoners were embarked and handed over to the police in Oban Harbour. They were, of course, suspects from a vessel involved in drugs traffic and intercepted by the warship.

Sadly, scarcely a year passes without the lifeboat being involved in the search for a body or bodies. On 30 November a 17-ft local creel boat operated by one young man was reported overdue and the lifeboat launched at 2017. Working a wide area in and around the Firth of Lorne as the missing man usually did, the search area was extensive and several other boats joined in as did helicopters. The search area was narrowed somewhat when a fleet of creels appearing to be freshly baited was found at Camus Nathais and, just after midnight, a helicopter reported a dinghy awash in the same area. The lifeboat closed the dinghy and found the fuel tanks empty, the choke "out" and no sign of a lifejacket. The fleet of creels was lifted and found to be clear. The search was called off until daylight on 1 December when various vessels, a police helicopter, an RAF helicopter and the lifeboat resumed it. Police and coastguard carried out shore searches but also without success and, reluctantly as always in these vexed circumstances, searching was discontinued.

The new year of 1991 was only five days old when an Isle of Mull doctor considered it advisable to have a maternity case transferred to hospital in Oban – pick-up at Craignure, Mull was arranged for 1900 hours and a doctor (lifeboat crewmember), midwife and incubator also taken along. Although the outward run took place in a fresh westerly wind of Force 4/5 and the pregnant mum embarked without problems, conditions in Oban Bay on return had deteriorated badly with the wind now north-westerly and ranging between Force 8-11. The patient and midwife were disembarked at 1953 and taken to hospital immediately by ambulance but the lifeboat was not re-moored and ready for service again until 2116 hours – this delay due to the extreme weather conditions prevailing in the bay and, of course, bringing also potential danger to the crew coming ashore in an inflatable dinghy – they made it, but "what price the new berth?" – again!

Two services, four days apart, later in January were, strangely enough, both medivacs and both from the island of Kerrera. In each case the patient had to be carried a fair distance in a stretcher and, therefore, maximum crew was taken. Weather conditions were favourable and the jobs went like clockwork. By now, the "mutiny" was over, the new berth was nearing completion and almost ready to be used. So far, it has been described in this book only as "the new berth" without any reference to its whereabouts or design. In an attempt to simplify this, let us say a small bay, deep enough to float the lifeboat (and perhaps a vessel of somewhat greater draught), was dredged out adjacent to the lifeboat station and sheltered from the west and north west by a massive wall along whose "inside" was constructed a slipway. Not only was disembarking (particularly stretcher cases) now possible in all conditions but, on launching, the crew no longer had to make the time-consuming row out to the mooring in sometimes dangerous conditions but merely descended a ladder on the berth wall. The lifeboat was moored clear of both sides of the "bay" by chains which when dropped, allowed the boat to fall in alongside. At the head of the berth a fuel store was built and all the services required – water, power and fuel – are now at hand on the slip.

The first service on which the new berth and slip were used took place on 5 March 1991 when the lifeboat arranged to rendezvous with Tobermory lifeboat off Lochaline and took over a patient from the island of Coll who had suffered a broken wrist. A smooth and comfortable disembarkation took place at the new facility – a real boon and blessing after years of poor landing facilities.

The summer of 1991 saw the usual variety of routine tows of broken-down and grounded vessels, medivacs and "pregivacs" – none of them "stretching" the lifeboat or her crew.

A slightly more awkward service, however, took place on 21 September 1991 at 0200 hours when the GP at Lochaline requested the transfer of a patient with a suspected coronary attack to Oban hospital. The patient lived in a cottage about a mile off the main road with only a track leading to it so some carrying over rough terrain and crossing of a burn was involved. No pier, jetty nor slip was available and the lifeboat was anchored as close to the shore as possible but still a considerable way out. On arrival, conditions for transfer were found not to be good. Crewmember (and now station honorary medical advisor) Dr Colin Wilson was taken ashore in the inflatable dinghy with stretcher, blankets and ambulance pouch, the dinghy returning to the boat when veering lines were rigged to help recover the dinghy, patient, doctor and other crewman. The SSE onshore wind had freshened to between Force 4 and 6 but, by quarter past four, all were aboard, the veering lines recovered and the lifeboat on her way back to Oban. As Captain MacLeod recorded, "A sound, seamanlike service performed by all concerned".

The final social event of 1991 took place on 7 December when the modernised lifeboat house was formally opened. Branch chairman, Lake Falconer, welcomed some 50 guests including the Institution's director, Lt Cdr Brian Miles and his wife, Anne together with Mr Bob McCutcheon and Mr Alastair Wright of Strathclyde Regional Council Estates Department who had been largely instrumental in bringing about the lease of the building to the RNLI. The director spoke briefly and declared the facilities open.

The winter of 1991/92 (November-March) saw nine launches but none of particular note. A service on 3 June 1992 involved a powered pleasure craft, which had major hydraulic problems and had 37 persons on board. The lifeboat took over from a fish farm workboat towing the casualty, lashed alongside and secured her alongside Taynuilt Pier.

The two couples and two children from Edinburgh enjoying a walk on the island of Kerrera on 19 July would have had no idea, as they set out, that they would, before long, be at the heart of a sea rescue. A fishing boat, with two persons aboard, had filled and sunk (cause unknown) off the south end of the island of Kerrera leaving the two men in the water. As the two struggled ashore (one in a poor state) they were assisted by the walkers, one of whom ran to telephone the coastguard from one of the only two cottages in this remote corner of the island. The others lit a fire on the shore and put their own warm clothes on the survivors. On the lifeboat's arrival, she was updated on the situation and requested a nearby yacht to stand by until the casualties were recovered. One lifeboat crewmember went ashore in the dinghy and recovered the two men to the lifeboat for a speedy transfer to an ambulance waiting at Port Beag slip. She then returned to the scene to pick up the remaining crew, the four adults and two children. Without the vigilance and quick, sensible actions of the walkers (one of whose forebears had lived on Kerrera), it is doubtful whether these two men would have survived. They received a well-deserved letter of thanks from the director of the RNLI.

The outcome of a traditional "puffer" carrying 130 tons of tarry chips running aground on the Falls of Lora would be difficult to forecast. This did occur on 20 August 1992 and the lifeboat was launched to stand-by until the puffer had refloated on the flood tide. This she did successfully and was piloted/escorted by the lifeboat until through the Dunstaffnage narrows.

Although the Institution exists primarily to "preserve life from shipwreck", this definition has the widest interpretation. The merest chance of any problem which could result in the loss of life will see a lifeboat launched – even if only anxiety on the part of the skipper is evident – for this, itself, might lead to problems. On 26 August a chartered motor-sailor with two adults and two small children aboard advised the coastguard that they were experiencing difficulties in the tide rips off Lismore Light. The lifeboat was launched and stood by the boat until she was safely through the bad patch and able to proceed on her own. A simple task for a lifeboat but probably a prayer answered for the skipper and crew of the motor-sailor.

If ever there was an example of the need to be clear, concise and un-ambiguous in the transmitting of a distress message, it was on 21 October 1992 when Oban Coastguard received a garbled message from an un-named vessel. The signal was very poor but the words "mayday", "on rocks", "engine failure" and "Ardmaddy" were picked up. It was not known whether this was Ardmaddy, Seil Sound or Ardmaddy, Loch Etive, which were in entirely opposite directions from Oban. The casualty, of course, may have sent a full and accurate position but neither the lifeboat, the fishing boat searching Seil Sound at the coastguard's request nor the RN Sea King helicopter also searching, found any sign of a vessel in distress in either position. During the service, which lasted about four hours, a message was received that a vessel had been sighted on rocks west of Luing – here again, nothing was found. Another report was received that a small fishing boat working near Ardmaddy, Loch Etive had not returned to her mooring as expected and the helicopter searched that area without success – soon after, this small fishing boat was reported safe and back on her mooring and the search called off. It is unthinkable that any vessel would use the word "mayday" loosely when her difficulties were not that serious. In the unlikely event that this was the case here, not only would there have been an abuse of rescue services' time and money as well as a loss of fishing time for the vessel asked to search, but a Search and Rescue helicopter and a lifeboat would have been already committed to a fruitless search should a genuine distress call have been received during these four hours.

Anyone who has forgotten their reading glasses when they have gone to, say, a choir practice or to make a speech, will surely sympathise with the skipper of a 35-ft fishing boat bound from Mallaig to Oban when he became unsure of his position in heavy showers and poor visibility. With no glasses or the "wrong" glasses, he was unable to read the chart and, wisely, called the coastguard and the lifeboat met him some 8 miles from Oban to escort him in!

On 4 December the lifeboat was asked to search the shoreline and bay following the finding of clothing on the shore belonging to a male just after he had had a "domestic row". The search began just after midday but was called off about an hour later when the police reported that the missing man was safe, having contacted not only his lodgings but also the Job Centre!

Some 999 calls are made in good faith when the situation is not at all serious. The caller on this occasion reported what appeared to be the sole male occupant of a small boat waving his arms while the boat went round in circles – this in Loch Etive. On her way to the loch the lifeboat was informed that the small boat was now proceeding up the loch and appeared to be OK. To ensure all was well, however, the lifeboat carried on to contact the boat only to find the occupant fishing happily – he had merely been waving to his wife as she passed in the car. The 999 caller had done the right thing, nevertheless.

Before 1992 had ended, yet another tragedy, which might have been avoided, occurred in the Sound of Kerrera. The report from the coastguard stated that a dinghy with outboard, one person aboard, working creels had sunk off the Kerrera ferry slip. Seven minutes after launching the lifeboat located the empty dinghy and the creels but no sign of the person and suggested that divers be called. The Cal Mac ferry *Lord of the Isles* and other vessels joined in the search while a helicopter from Prestwick was also requested. A lifeboat crewmember in the "X" boat (a small inflatable) searched the shoreline. By 1500 hours the divers had located the body of the missing man – who was found not to be wearing a lifejacket – and the lifeboat transferred it and the dinghy into police hands.

CHAPTER V

1993-1993

The Brede Years (iii)

The new year of 1993 opened on no happier a note when, on 9 January, a young lady canoeist died in an accident on the River Awe. She had been one of two in a double canoe, which came to grief as they paddled it down river to Loch Etive. Her partner managed to scramble ashore but there was no sign of the girl even after the rear section of the canoe was found near the scene of the accident. A helicopter, the lifeboat and many shore-walkers took part in the search. A decision was taken to open the Hydro Board barrage, which separates Loch Awe from the River Awe, and the lifeboat stood by at the river mouth. This produced no result and the search was scaled down until dawn. The helicopter, in any case, had been grounded earlier after touching a power line with her tail rotor – luckily she suffered no real damage and no one was hurt. The search was resumed next morning and the lifeboat recovered the body of the young woman from a small island off Bonawe Quarry almost straight away. With little depth at Taynuilt Pier and a southerly wind touching Force 7 at times, the body was taken back to Oban.

More successful, albeit not until the following day, was the service for which the relief lifeboat *Enid of Yorkshire* was launched on 27 February when a 20-ft creel boat with two persons aboard was reported overdue – she was the *Three Sisters*. A wide search was carried out from Bonawe to Bogha Nuadh and taking on board, for a time, a crewmember normally on the *Three Sisters* so that he might indicate where their creels were usually laid. The search was suspended just after midnight and resumed at 0700 next morning. Within 40 minutes the fishing vessel *Golden Opportunity* reported having picked up the missing men who were transferred to the lifeboat off the north end of Kerrera and landed in Oban to an ambulance for hospital.

Later that morning, when now on exercise, the lifeboat was advised that three crewmembers of the 45-ft fishing vessel *Golden West* were marooned on a small reef off Puilldobhrainn. Their boat had sunk around 1700 hours the previous evening leaving them to swim to this reef. Huddled together there, they hoped that the fire they had lit on the boat before she sank had been seen by somebody. They were convinced that help was on its way when they saw a vessel's lights and a searchlight nearby – ironically these were the lights of the lifeboat searching for the *Three Sisters* referred to in the previous service! With no sign of help at all, one of the four decided he would swim for the shore and after a long, difficult struggle over creeks and rocks, he staggered into the Tigh an Truish Inn to raise the alarm. This was the message that reached the lifeboat on exercise at 1102 and, within 40 minutes, the remaining three survivors were on board and heading for Oban where they were transferred by ambulance to hospital. All four recovered fully despite spending a February night wet and cold on a tiny reef in the Firth of Lorne. Such was the interest in their story that the BBC featured it later in their *999* series narrated by Michael Buerk.

The invaluable benefit of having a doctor on the lifeboat crew was well illustrated on 1 March when an injured seaman on a fishing vessel was brought ashore to hospital. On the short run in, Gordon Murchison attended to the laceration from eye to scalp by washing it out with seawater, inserting five staples and applying a pressure bandage.

In many services, the lifeboat appears to the "man in the street" to have had the final rescue snatched from her by a helicopter or other vessel. Nothing could be further from the truth. On 5 April 1993, a yacht with two persons aboard reported engine failure south of Shuna, Melfort, feared she would strike rocks and was launching her liferaft. A further report stated that she had struck the rocks, the water was up to chart table level and she was listing some 45 degrees.

Communications then ceased indicating that the yachtsmen had almost certainly taken to the liferaft. The helicopter, now on scene, spotted a red flare and flew directly to it, indicating that she would attempt to lift the two survivors from the liferaft – this she did and flew them to Connel. The lifeboat returned to Oban – job successfully completed by our colleagues from the SAR squadron at RN, Prestwick. All that matters is that any lives in danger are saved but it is true to say that all members of the Search and Rescue "family" like to be "hands on" at the conclusion of a service!

All fishing boats like to return to port with something in their nets but one vessel got more than she bargained for on 27 April 1993. Coastguard reported that she had a torpedo in her net and its forward section on the foredeck. Naval authorities at Rosyth requested lifeboat assistance and the Brede *Nottinghamshire* (which had now replaced the *Ann Ritchie*) duly embarked three MOD personnel and landed them aboard the fishing boat. The bomb disposal team did what was necessary, lowering the warhead to the seabed where it was exploded safely.

Apart from the usual medivacs and pregivacs from islands or vessels, calls during the rest of the year included the evacuation of a wife and small child from a boat aground at the mouth of Loch Feochan, the vessel itself being towed off by an Ardoran Marine workboat. The *Nottinghamshire* also ferried six firemen out to the unmanned Lismore Lighthouse when it was thought fire had broken out – only to discover that the flames and smoke emanated from a fire of garden rubbish, which the tenants in the former lighthouse cottage had lit!

A pleasure boat operating out of Oban lost all power on 9 July when on the west side of the island of Kerrera and with 14 persons on board. The lifeboat had the casualty in tow within 14 minutes of the call and 14 relieved people (and the skipper) were brought safely into Oban.

The long cliff-girt south coast of the island of Mull can be an intimidating place especially as darkness falls and more especially in a yacht without power in light winds and in the hands of an inexperienced crew. The four occupants were, therefore, mightily relieved on 21 July when the lifeboat took their vessel in tow to Carsaig Bay where the lifeboat crew saw her safely anchored.

On 26 July 1993 an 18-ft speedboat was reported overdue on a trip from Balvicar to the west side of Jura having been expected back in Balvicar the previous evening. Islay lifeboat had been launched, a Fishery Protection aircraft was assisting and Oban lifeboat was launched at 1106. Arriving on scene, Oban lifeboat was directed to the casualty by a fishing boat and began escorting her back to Balvicar but temporarily left her in order to assess conditions in the Gulf of Corriebhreacan. The south side was considered to be too rough for the speedboat and the escort continued by hugging the Scarba (or north) shore. Soon after, the casualty signalled she was happy with the situation and set course for Balvicar, the *Nottinghamshire* returning to Oban.

On 2 August 1993, the large fishing vessel *Hebron* grounded on Lady Rock, off Lismore Light, the forefoot being some 3 ft above water level. On the arrival of the lifeboat, this time under the command of Second Coxswain Douglas Craig, four crewmembers of the *Hebron* were taken aboard. The fishing vessel *Silver Dawn* arrived to assist and, with aid of the lifeboat, put a line aboard the *Hebron*. In her first attempt to refloat the casualty, however, *Silver Dawn* slewed and grounded herself. The lifeboat was able to tow her off and the line from *Silver Dawn* to *Hebron* was re-established. With the lifeboat holding her bow up-tide, *Silver Dawn* then succeeded in re-floating the *Hebron* and the lifeboat towed her successfully to Oban – five hours after the first call.

The second coxswain was kept busy about now for, only five days later, he was in command again when the *Nottinghamshire* was called to the assistance of the yacht *Extrovert,* with six persons aboard, taking part in a race of West Highland Week. She had struck the rock south of Kerrera known as Dubh Sgeir and was taking water fast. Other vessels were standing by the casualty but an open "carrier" on Channel 16 was hindering communications. On scene, the lifeboat reported that only some 3 or 4 ft of

Extrovert's transom was above water and feared that she was beyond assistance. Sure enough, at 1500 hours the lifeboat reported "Casualty has sunk". All on board had earlier been taken off by the Regatta Committee vessel *Green Pastures.* The open "carrier" on Channel 16 had now ceased and had, most likely, been on the casualty.

Despite the unbelievable view of the coastguard that the incident was not "maritime", a discussion between coxswain and launching authority resulted in Oban lifeboat launching on 18 August 1993 to search the shores of the island of Scarba for two persons missing overnight from an adventure school on the island. The strong possibility that one or both of the missing persons had fallen or found their way to a part of the shore accessible only by sea meant that their evacuation might only be by boat. In the event, the missing persons (cold but uninjured) were located by the lifeboat, taken aboard and returned to Oban.

A fleet of Oban Sailing Club dinghies, manned by teenagers, was devastated on the evening of 2 September when a sudden squall swept through Oban Bay. The lifeboat crew, still on board following engine trials with the divisional engineer, responded immediately and took aboard five young persons between the ages of 12-15, landing them at the lifeboat berth. By this time, a request from Dr Bill Clegg of Tobermory, Isle of Mull for the evacuation of a critically ill patient had been received and, as soon as Crewmember Dr Colin Wilson arrived with drugs and equipment the *Nottinghamshire* left to pick up the patient at the linkspan at Craignure. Despite continuous attention by the doctor, the patient died on the way to Oban.

Before the month was over, yet another fishing vessel had reason to be thankful to Oban Lifeboat. Just after midnight on 9 September 1993, the fishing vessel *Alkaid* was reported aground on the reef Sgeir Rathaid in Oban Bay and the lifeboat launched to her assistance just before 1am. Several attempts to tow her off immediately were unsuccessful and, after putting a salvage pump aboard the casualty as a precaution, the lifeboat returned to the station arranging to relaunch at 0830 hours. *Alkaid* had been left firmly aground but stable. At 0937 the tide was considered to have come sufficiently for another attempt to be made. Taking a warp from the casualty, the lifeboat re-floated her at 0954 – no apparent damage having been sustained.

Hardly had the search for an overdue yacht been concluded on 13 September 1993 (the yacht had been traced to moorings at Ardsheal and all was well) when the *Nottinghamshire* was called to investigate a report of a red flare in the Sound of Jura. Topping up with fuel at Oban on the way south, the lifeboat proceeded to the Dorus Mor area where a speedboat with three persons aboard was overdue. At 2326 a red flare was sighted over Garbh Reisa, the lifeboat replying with a white parachute flare. Soon after, three people were seen on Garbh Reisa having opted to stay on the island when the tide had "beaten" them. All three were taken aboard the lifeboat, their boat taken in tow and the entire party landed at Crinan. The lifeboat was back in Oban, refuelled and ready for service again just before 2am the following morning, having been on service for a total of some seven hours.

On 14 November, while in the process of bringing a patient with a broken wrist off the island of Kerrera, coastguard reported four skin-divers being swept out to sea off Dunollie Point. The priority was not difficult to establish and, within seven minutes, all four divers were picked up and landed at the South Pier. The "broken wrist" patient was then taken aboard and transferred to an ambulance for the short trip to hospital.

Certain services come under the heading of "compassionate" and one such took place on 22 November 1993. A request was received from the then County Hospital, Oban to convey the wife of a seriously ill patient to Oban from the Isle of Mull from where her husband had been transferred by lifeboat the previous evening. The hospital now considered the patient's life to be in imminent danger. The transfer was made and the lady was in the hospital before her husband, sadly, died later in the day. Decisions of this kind fall upon the Hon. Sec. or his deputy launching authorities at the station, the "pros" on this occasion being, not only the compassionate nature of the request, but the fact that substantial support of the RNLI is received from the people of Mull. Little difficulty was found in agreeing to this one. The Institution will not be the losers.

CHAPTER VI

1994-1997

The Brede Years (iv)

The year 1994 began with a service to the head of Loch Etive on 23 January to investigate the finding of a 13-ft rowing boat, oars and rowlocks on the shore. The first informant believed the boat to belong to the owner of a holiday cottage on the loch and that it was securely stored in a locked outbuilding. Theft was, therefore, suspected and fairly well confirmed when the cottage concerned was found to have been ransacked.

Another of these "double" services took place on 7/8 April when a 75-ft converted Brixham trawler went aground in Puilladobhrainn anchorage with 16 persons on board. The lifeboat was launched with a portable pump aboard, which the second coxswain and one crewmember took on board the casualty. The ingress of water was stemmed and the decision taken to evacuate ten persons to Oban returning to stand by the casualty's attempt to re-float around 1500 hours. By 1730, all attempts to re-float her were unsuccessful and, as soon as the casualty was seen to have settled, further attempts were delayed until next morning at about 4am. By 0450 the fishing vessel was afloat and considered seaworthy allowing the lifeboat to return to station where she was ready for service again at 0541 hours.

Another call in the category of "false alarm with good intent" took place on 28 April 1994 when a member of the public reported having seen a person scrambling about the girders under Connel Bridge then disappearing. Fearing an attempted suicide, the coastguard requested the lifeboat launch to investigate. While in the search area, the lifeboat was informed that the person under the bridge had been a surveyor examining the structure – "better safe than sorry" as the saying goes.

On 29 June, the lifeboat coxswain instructed a small fishing boat, lying in the Sound of Kerrera with total machinery failure, to retrieve her anchor before securing the tow. Imagine his amazement when, at the end of the anchor cable, there was nothing more than a Black & Decker-type Workmate! The casualty was, of course, towed home safely.

A month later there was an example of how a simple service should be conducted for both the benefit of the casualty AND without upsetting the lobster fishermen involved. A 36-ft yacht had fouled her propeller and rudder in a fleet of creels. On arrival, the lifeboat crew cut and buoyed the fleet then, using the yacht's own dinghy, freed her propeller and rudder. They then re-attached the buoyed line to the creel fleet and all parties were happy!

The second half of 1994 saw a further 33 services including 13 medivacs, ten groundings of a variety of craft and a further ten miscellaneous calls including one to a large motor cruiser with five persons on board, suffering complete power failure off the Garvellach Islands in a WSW Force 5 and heavy swell. Within an hour of launching, the lifeboat had the casualty in tow for Easdale but the possible difficulty in berthing her there in the swell, resulted in altering course for Oban where the cruiser was secured on a mooring and her passengers landed, some three hours later.

Another call was in response to a report of an EPIRB signal coming from the region of Lismore Island/Sound of Mull. No vessel was located in trouble in the area but a SAR helicopter, departing after a completely unconnected search in Loch Sunart, had intercepted a weak EPIRB signal which was traced to a faulty EPIRB on a vessel in Loch Aline.

On 1 October 1994 a 14-m yacht with seven persons aboard lost all steering in the area of the Torran Rocks, south-west of Mull, the lifeboat meeting up with her some 6 miles east of the Torran Rocks – a rescue helicopter was also on scene and another yacht standing by. As she was 200 yds offshore the lifeboat advised her to drop anchor and a lifeboat crewman went aboard to assist in the setting up of emergency steering gear. After confirming that the casualty was answering properly to her emergency steering, the lifeboat returned to Oban.

In 1995 some 87 services took place, these being the usual mixture of vessels grounded, vessels overdue, persons in the water, divers overdue, divers separated from their mother ship, medivacs and pregivacs and many in the "one-off" category. The classic "bundle of clothes on the beach – suicide?" featured occasionally but never to any negative result.

Launches to pick up divers with suspected de-compression sickness or the "bends" and take them to the de-compression chamber at Dunstaffnage are fairly common. Not so well known, however, is that, occasionally the doctor (often a lifeboat crewmember who is also a doctor) remains with the patient until the treatment is completed. The doctor, thereby, commits himself for anything between five and sixty hours (sometimes IN the chamber) – this last figure being the time spent in the "pot" on one occasion by Crewmember Dr Colin Wilson who also accompanied the patient taken to Dunstaffnage by the lifeboat on 26 March.

No lifeboatman and no lifeboat official will ever complain that a call was un-necessary (unless, of course, in cases of deliberate hoax), but they have every right to expect that the vessels or persons in whose interests they have launched will co-operate by doing what they are asked to do by the lifeboat or the coastguard involved – there is always a good reason for the request. The casualty in one incident in April 1995, a diver swept away by tide in Loch Creran, did not. After managing to reach the shore, admittedly very tired, he was asked to remain there until the CG land-rover arrived. Coastguard advised that, on arrival, there was no sign of the diver nor of the shore party. Later it was established that the diver and his family had returned to their caravan ignoring the request. In a case like this, only when the SAR bodies are satisfied that reports of safe landing or return are beyond doubt, can they stand-down the vessels and vehicles involved.

The incident could not, therefore, be closed until much later because of the diver's behaviour.

Before April 1995 was out, two more skin divers' lives were lost while diving on a WWII wreck in Ardmucknish Bay, Benderloch, north of Oban. The lifeboat attended, the landing crewmember and "diving" doctor, Colin Wilson on the divers' mother-ship, the *Harry Slater* in readiness for the surfacing of the missing men. It was not to be, however, for the two divers were not recovered.

The WWII wreck, *Breda*, lies in Ardmucknish Bay, Benderloch and is a very popular site for skin-divers. The *Breda* was sunk by German bombers in 1940 as she lay in the anchorage with other merchantmen awaiting the arrival of the RN escort to accompany them across the Atlantic. Although not sustaining a direct hit, the *Breda* sustained fatal damage from a near-miss and, although making shallow water at first, she sank into 15 fathoms where she still lies. Her cargo of lorries, cement and small planes also included a number of racehorses, including one believed to belong to the Aga Khan.

Enjoyment for a young 14-year-old girl on holiday on the island of Scarba suddenly turned to anxiety on 30 May when she sustained a severe back injury while being towed on a "biscuit" by a high-powered launch. While turning, the "biscuit" hit the corner of a pontoon and the girl was thrown upwards and landed very badly thus damaging her back. She was placed in a basket stretcher on the lifeboat and was monitored closely by Crewmember Dr Colin Wilson who administered entonox when necessary on the fast passage to Oban. The waiting ambulance there transferred her to hospital.

One service on 28 June served as an example of how visitors to our shores fail to appreciate the strengths and variances of the tides. Three German tourists on a caravan holiday at North Ledaig, set out in a 10-ft inflatable dinghy for, it was thought, a fishing trip up Loch Etive at 1100. When they had failed to return by 2020 the owners of the caravan site alerted the lifeboat, which launched at 2023 only to meet the overdue dinghy coming through the Falls of Lora at Connel Bridge at

2052. All was well although it is doubtful whether the occupants had any inkling of the severe conditions that can be met in the Falls of Lora.

One almost humorous shout took place on 16 August when launching to assist a vessel reported to be on fire. A helicopter exercising with Mallaig lifeboat was diverted to investigate and identified the "casualty" as none other than the old puffer *Vic 32* making excessive smoke while flashing up!

The greatest number of persons taken aboard the lifeboat on a single service in 1995 was 14 – seven from each of two rigid inflatables from the Puffin Dive Centre that had broken down were adrift and in danger of being swamped. All were safely landed at Dunstaffnage on 8 October.

On the subject of examples, another occurred on 19 November when a 29-ft motor-sailor in difficulties just west of the Gulf of Corriebhreacan had been taken in tow by FV *Catriona* and then by the RN fleet tender *Ironbridge*. The lifeboat was then released to continue to search the area. Why? – because the number of red flares sighted amounted to more than the casualty reported having fired. Nothing more was found but, had the full search not been carried out, some poor vessel in trouble might have gone unheeded. Such is an example of how thoroughly the RNLI and the coastguard operate.

In 1996 there were 72 launches of which ten were false alarms and, of that figure, sadly some were thought to be hoaxes. Machinery failures accounted for the greatest cause of services with strandings, divers and diving boats coming close behind.

One of the largest vessels assisted by the relatively small 33-ft Brede lifeboat in 1996 was the 295-ton *Ronja Fisk,* a specialised fish-farm vessel registered in the Norwegian port of Alesund. She had gone aground on the Branra Rock on the east side of Lismore on an ebb tide and, after taking soundings around her, Coxswain Maclean advised the master to batten down the hatches and secure the vessel. After two hours the casualty had settled without further listing and the lifeboat returned to station to await higher tide. Some five hours later the lifeboat and two other vessels had lines aboard the *Ronja Fisk,* the lifeboat alternating between taking the strain and surging the towline in attempts to free the casualty, this succeeding after about 15 minutes. *Ronja Fisk* was making no water and returned to Oban for diver inspection.

When the phrase "person/s in the water" is heard, even greater than usual urgency attends any service. Such was the case on 26 April when a 20-year-old girl had fallen into the water at the North Pier and, although she had been pulled from the sea, the lifeboat was required to remove her from the staging under the pier and to the ambulance. She was found to be unconscious and hypothermic but breathing and, wrapped in blankets, she was in the care of the ambulance crew within nine minutes of the lifeboat launching.

The following day, one of the thankfully infrequent hoax calls appeared to take place. Two vessels and the coastguard all heard the word "mayday" spoken once by a male voice but not heard again and certainly not accompanied by the name and position of a vessel. The lifeboat launched at 1412 and searched the west side of Kerrera, Bach Island, Loch Feochan mouth, Puilladobhrainn, Ardencaple and as far as Cullipool, Isle of Luing – finding no vessel in trouble. These despicable calls are, of course, a waste of RNLI money and of crews' time.

Exactly one month later, a call for assistance from the yacht *Borealis* was certainly no hoax. She had had the misfortune to run aground on a nasty little rock north of Innish Island off Easdale Island. When the lifeboat arrived on scene the yacht was taking water and, after assessing the situation, Coxswain Pat Maclean requested that a salvage pump be brought by road to Easdale where it was picked up by *Kingfisher* and transferred to the lifeboat. It was immediately put to work on the casualty and a second pump requested as a precaution – this pump was delivered by the coastguard but, in fact, not used. Ardfern Yacht Centre was requested to prepare their travel hoist for the yacht, which it was hoped could be kept afloat and towed in to Ardfern. Meantime, Alasdair Maclean and Maitland Black, both boat-builders, volunteered their services in an attempt to make temporary repairs to *Borealis'* hull and were taken out by Bruce Smith, Lerags, in his rib.

They were, however, unable to improve the situation and returned to Ardfern with the lifeboat. Just before 11 p.m. *Borealis* floated and was towed to Ardfern by the lifeboat with the salvage pump still operating, reaching the Marina at 1.15am. She was slipped by 1.45am, the lifeboat recovered the pumps and gear and returned to Oban where she was made ready for service again by 0418 hours. To quote Captain Norman MacLeod, the hon sec, "There is no doubt that, but for lifeboat action, this yacht would have been a total loss" – sentiments with which the yacht's owners themselves readily agree.

The pump used was of the type known as a "trash" pump, which can pass solids as well as water, dispensing with the need, periodically, to stop operations and open up the hose in order to clear, for example, seaweed – a not unusual item to find in the bilges of a vessel opened up to the sea. The marine insurance company Sunderland Marine had, earlier, made a gift of this pump to Oban Lifeboat at the suggestion of marine surveyor, Bruce Smith, he being convinced that it would, one day, prevent a claim for the total loss of at least one vessel which that company insured. And so it proved to be – on 7 August 1996 a 17-m fishing vessel ran aground near the Corran Narrows and was making water. The lifeboat's pump was put aboard and set in motion, pumping the boat dry and keeping her afloat until the lifeboat towed her off near high water and escorted her safely to Corpach. For interest, Coxswain Maclean asked the casualty's skipper "with which company are you insured?" "Sunderland Marine" came the answer!

After considerable pressure from the station, HQ finally agreed to fit a second searchlight on the Brede, the lack of another having proved restrictive during some night services. The first service on which the second light was reported upon very favourably took place in Easdale Sound when a 40-ton Bristol Channel pilot cutter, with eight persons aboard, dragged her anchor and was pinned against a shoal in a SSE wind of Force 5/6 and tide of up to 3.5 knots. The lifeboat arrived on scene at 0245, pulled the casualty clear and, using the two searchlights to illuminate both sides of the narrow channel simultaneously, conned the Cutter out into deep water from where she proceeded on her passage to Duart Bay.

For the lifeboat crew to have a laugh at the expense of those picked up or towed home is seldom the case but such it was on 7 July when a 26-ft power boat, with four persons on board, broke down on her way from Mull to Oban. The tow home was straightforward but hardly amusing until it was revealed that one of the "survivors" was the coxswain of Tobermory Lifeboat on his way to RNLI, Poole for a training course!

Co-operation with another lifeboat station on a more serious note occurred a few days later when a helicopter, tasked to pick up a 60-year-old diver on the island of Islay with suspected "bends", was unable to land due to dense fog. In view of the man's age and the possible serious consequences of delay, it was decided to rendezvous with Islay Lifeboat and transfer the patient to the Oban boat. This was duly done, the transfer taking place some 22 miles southwest of Oban and the patient disembarked to an ambulance in Oban at 0343 hours.

Medical services seemed to be the flavour of the month when a "double" took place on 11 July with the evacuation from Mull of a 6-month-old baby suffering from suspected meningitis along with a young boy thought to have appendicitis. The asset of having a doctor on the crew was appreciated more than ever since no time need be lost in finding one who was able and willing to attend and in view of the fact that two patients required attention – the appendix case needing monitoring while the baby's IV fluids had to be continued, anti-convulsants and oxygen administered.

Before the month was out another very worthwhile service was carried out. A 46-ft twin-engined motor-cruiser of the "Nelson" type, named *Lady Blue*, sustained serious damage with drastic "domino" effect. Just after clearing the Torran Rocks bound Oban, the skipper increased speed to his normal cruising level of 17/18 knots only to hear an ominous "thud" which, it was established later, was the sound of three of the four starboard engine mounts shearing allowing that engine to swing, severing the prop shaft. The "freed" prop shaft quickly tore the stern gland out and then sheared off the starboard rudder. To quote the owner/skipper, "copious quantities of water" then flooded the engine room! Further hull damage occurred by shaft rotation, which it was found impossible to overcome at speeds in excess of 4.5 knots.

An SAR helicopter and Oban lifeboat were immediately launched in answer to the mayday from the casualty. The lifeboat arrived on scene at 1900 hours, the SAR helicopter's winchman already on board the motor-cruiser and the aircraft standing by. The casualty's crew comprised the skipper and his wife, both experienced sailors, together with their King Charles spaniel. The lifeboat's engineer and two crewmembers were landed aboard with a salvage pump. Arrangements were made for Ardfern Yacht Centre to prepare to slip the vessel, ETA at Ardfern being 0000 hours, and the casualty began the slow passage (at about 4.5 knots) to Ardfern via the Gulf of Corriebhreacan. The helicopter recovered her winchman and was released, the casualty, escorted by the lifeboat, leaving the scene for Loch Craignish at 1934 hours.

At 2230 Lifeboat Crewman Colin Wilson (also a doctor trained in diving medicine) was recalled to attend a diving casualty at Oban and was landed by the lifeboat at Ardfern, picked up by locally based crewman, Angus Ritchie, and driven to Kilmelford where Station Hon Sec Norman MacLeod took him on to Oban. The lifeboat returned to the casualty whose pump and speed were still a successful combination and, at 2356 she was slipped as arranged.

The skipper of a small sailing boat being pounded by a westerly wind and sea against the Railway Pier in Oban Bay on 4 October had been taken off with difficulty up on to the pier but having to leave his two dogs stranded on board. The lifeboat launching authority was asked to consider assisting in their recovery and readily agreed – after all, the RNLI's original name was "The National Association for the Preservation of <u>Life</u> from Shipwreck" – no mention of restricting it to human life! Between a crewmember landed on the pier and those on board, the two animals were brought ashore safely.

For some years now, an elderly gentleman has lived for several months of each year in a cave on the small island of Innis off Easdale, making radio contact at fortnightly intervals to confirm his well-being. On 30 October his scheduled broadcast was not received and the lifeboat was launched to investigate, taking two coastguards along with them. The RNLI is always happy to take members of the coastguard afloat when circumstances allow it, the feeling being that the more the coastguard are aware of what a lifeboat's problems can be, the better equipped they will be at their desks. All was found to be well, the only problem being flat batteries in the gentleman's VHF radio.

Seafarers worldwide, like car drivers, are used to the "infallibility" of signals – until, that is, the failure of traffic lights at a busy junction or the failure of a lighthouse on the coast – inevitable from time to time. A large fishing vessel became confused in the area of Lismore Light on 8 November 1996 when that beacon ceased to function and the lifeboat was launched to escort her through the narrows until she was happy with her course up the Sound of Mull.

Six containers were washed overboard in the North Atlantic on 18 December 1996 from a ship bound for Liverpool. Where does Oban Lifeboat come in? Well, one of the "do we launch – do we not launch" situations arose when the hon sec was asked if he would authorise the ferrying of a specialist chemist and two firemen to the Isle of Mull at 0030 hours on 6 March 1997. When it was explained that the 5-ton container contained dangerous tetra-ethyl lead and had washed up on the shore at Ulva Ferry on the west side of Mull with a possible consequent risk to life, the launch was agreed and the three men with breathing equipment duly ferried over to the island.

Two calls within three weeks of each other in April both related, in a vague way, to electronic aids to navigation. The first failed when a 10-m vessel without radar or Decca reported that she was unsure of her position and had no charts of the area. The lifeboat found her in an unexpected position and escorted her into Oban. It was suspected that an electrical or electronic failure in her plotter had occurred. The second incident involved a report that a Search and Rescue satellite "hit" showed a possible location of the signal as the Benderloch area. Shortly after launching, some doubt was reported as to the possible location but the lifeboat was requested to circumnavigate the Isle of Lismore. One hour after the initial call the "hit" was identified as being Dyce Airport, Aberdeen! Modern electronics are not infallible. The message? – in the first case, have paper charts on the chart table and in the second, keep an open mind.

On 8 June 1997 the skipper of a yacht fell overboard when the boat suffered a knock-down in the Firth of Lorne, sustaining a head injury in the process. The remaining crewmembers managed to get him back aboard and she was taken in tow by a nearby yacht. Conditions were not good and little progress was being made. On the lifeboat's arrival, Crewmember Dr Colin Wilson made a mammoth leap on to the casualty taking a tow rope with him. He then attended to the injured skipper who was transferred to the lifeboat along with the rest of the yacht's crew. The assisting yacht was released and the lifeboat took the casualty to a mooring in Dallens Bay, Appin before transferring the injured skipper to hospital in Oban.

A service which began on 15 June, effectively ended only on 20 June. This was the tragic case of a diver working with a group on a wreck west of the island of Belnahua, one of the "slate" islands southwest of Easdale Island. Prior to the arrival of lifeboat and SAR helicopter, one of the group of divers, with suspected decompression sickness, had already been landed to an ambulance at Cuan slipway.

With numerous vessels assisting in the search, the lifeboat was appointed "on scene commander" while the naval diving tender *Instow* with divers aboard, was proceeding from Oban and Islay Lifeboat coming north from Port Askaig at maximum speed. Meantime, the dive vessel *Porpoise* stood by the "shot" buoy.

"It never rains but it pours" goes the saying – at 1912 hours Crewmember Dr Colin Wilson was requested to attend an emergency at Oban Hospital and was airlifted by the SAR helicopter to Oban, the aircraft returning with Crewmember David Graham as his replacement. At 2134 hours all units were released with a resumption of the search arranged for 0600 hours the following morning. The search continued as planned with Oban and Islay Lifeboats, *Urchin* and *Puffin 2* all involved but, only on 20 June, did a naval remote control machine from the RMAS *Cockchafer* locate the diver's body.

The baby girl who accidentally swallowed lighter fluid on 15 July 1997 on the island of Kerrera could not have known that she was the reason for the last launch of a Brede lifeboat from Oban Station. On the way to Kerrera to pick up the baby the lifeboat met the baby girl and her parents on the way to Oban in an outboard dinghy and directed them to the lifeboat slip where either a car or ambulance would be awaiting. She made a good recovery.

Berth - Before

Berth - During

Berth - After

Norman MacLeod receiving the M.B.E from The Queen

"Dorothy and Philip Constant" on her mooring in N.W.Gale

"Oops!"

Pat with crew on his retiral
(courtesy of Stewart Fair)

Emma Cato – Just born on board!

"Ann Ritchie" naming ceremony

"Watkin Williams" and I.L.B at South Pier, Oban.

The Station's first raft race crew.

Patrick Maclean   Gordon Murchison   Malcolm Robertson

The Inventors of "V.I.T.A.L."

"Watkin Williams" exercising with helicopter – 1980
(Courtesy of Kenny Keane)

Colin Wilson leaping aboard a yacht to treat the injured skipper

"Shemara" on Lady Rock
(Courtesy of Bruce Smith)

The original South Pier "sheds"

The present station

Oban distillery manager, Ian Williams, wishing the Trent "Good luck."

The Hans Gude painting

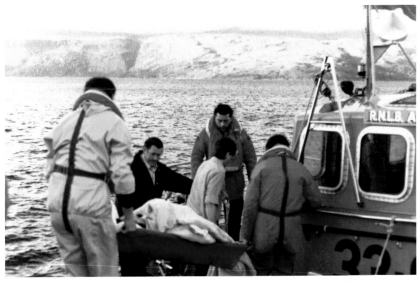

Embarking a patient at Craignure, Isle of Mull

The "delivery" crew wetting the baby's head

Crew at the "Mora Edith MacDonald" naming ceremony

Radio training caravan

On the "Branra" Rock

Elaine Mulgrew – the "balloon" girl

The present chief of operations in more junior days

The crew and wives taken to dinner by Mrs Ann Ritchie – 1983

"Twirly" Thomson demonstrating splicing during a Malt 'n' Salt weekend

Portpatrick lifeboat escorting Oban Watson into Portpatrick
(Courtesy of David Graham)

Starting line of the raft race from a Sea King helicopter

Portpatrick lifeboat escorting Oban Watson into Portpatrick
(Courtesy of David Graham)

Paying respects to H.M The Queen as "Britannia" passed Duart
Castle

Launching in the early days

The Brede and Wessex helicopter

The Watson

The Brede

Working with helicopters

Marshall MacKinnon by his pool – Malt 'n' Salt weekend

Patrick Maclean receiving the M.B.E from The Queen

Sir Jimmy Savile

The Brede off Lismore

"Classic Wave" – Aground
(Courtesy of Ian Henry)

"Classic Wave" – Awash
(Courtesy of Ian Henry)

"Classic Wave" – Sunk
(Courtesy of Ian Henry)

The cask-end

Cox'n Ronnie MacKillop at the helm of the Trent
(Courtesy of Dennis Hardley)

Fundraisers

Norman and "The Barrel"

Ronnie MacKillop and Billy Forteith

Wilson Scott in the I.L.B

Duke of Kent's visit – 1980

"Mora Edith MacDonald" in Oban Bay
(Courtesy of Tony Hardley)

CHAPTER VII

1997-2004

The Trent Years

The arrival of a new lifeboat at any station is always a cause for comparisons but exceptionally so when the lifeboat is of a different CLASS. Thus it was on 16 July 1997 when the 14-m Trent-class lifeboat arrived in Oban to replace the 33-ft Brede. She was the *Mora Edith Macdonald,* funded by the generous bequest of Miss Mora Edith Macdonald together with the bequests of Mrs Janet Boyd Finlay-Maclean, Mrs Harriet Elizabeth Willis Gaunt and Mrs Annie Thomson Hart.

Her arrival was colourful and noisy. The "old" boat, the *Nottinghamshire,* dressed overall and carrying a piper welcomed the new boat, also dressed, in the Sound of Kerrera and, accompanied by other craft of all kinds, entered the Bay, each trying to outdo her neighbours with sound signals. As the two vessels came bow-to-bow off the North Pier, Ian Williams, manager of Oban Distillery, poured a dram of Oban Malt over the Trent's bows for good luck – the formal christening and naming ceremony was to take place much later – on 23 May 1998.

The Trent's first service was not a happy one. On 27 July an empty dinghy with outboard engine in gear and an empty fuel tank was found in Loch Creran. The dinghy was believed to belong to a crewmember of a large motor-cruiser nearby but, despite a thorough search of the loch by both lifeboat and helicopter, no one was found. The helicopter was released and the lifeboat continued searching for the next three hours again with nothing found. On 11 August the lifeboat assisted the police in the recovery of a body believed to be that of the missing man.

The medical reasons for patients having to be evacuated either from islands or vessels are usually fairly commonplace – such as appendicitis, pregnancy or heart attack. On 31 July, however, the lady evacuated to hospital in Oban suffering from abdominal pain had swallowed an "AA" battery – a first! While still on medical evacuations, the service on 5 August to transport a lady in labour from Mull to hospital in Oban started off as many similar others had done over the years – a midwife with incubator on board. The patient and her husband were embarked at Craignure and the midwife, Mrs Joanne Thorpe, assisted by the crew when necessary, attended the mother throughout. On reaching Oban Bay, however, Mrs Thorpe considered that labour was too far advanced to transfer the patient to the waiting ambulance and, on reaching the berth, a second midwife, Mrs Mairi MacGregor came aboard to assist. The lifeboat's return of service then reads "0901 – It's a girl!" For the next few days, the crew involved faced the Press continuously and Second Coxswain Douglas Craig (in command during the coxswain's holidays), a bachelor, looked pretty pleased! As the hon sec said at the time "A memorable first for Oban Lifeboat crew – the excitement of the birth of Hazel Beth Mora Banner will long be remembered. It was pleasing for us all that the name Mora was included". Connection with the Banner family has been maintained since (indeed, Hazel Beth and her parents were guests at the Trent's naming ceremony in 1998) and the station periodically receives photographs of Hazel as she grows up.

As already said, there is no length to which a lifeboat will not go to save "life". An extract from a return of service in August reads "…children, with their hamster, transferred to lifeboat". They were being transferred as a result of their parents' yacht having gone aground on the rock at Rubh Garbh-aird, Ardmucknish Bay. The parents remained aboard and, with the help of several other vessels who had answered the mayday, the lifeboat gently towed the casualty off, the skipper confirming that all seemed well apart from some possible damage to the transducer.

Later in August the lifeboat was called to the assistance of a woman in the sea, attempting to escape from the police. Within six minutes the lifeboat was recalled, the woman having returned to the shore – perhaps the water was too cold? On 5 September, what was thought to be a hoax call brought the Brede out of "hibernation" to join the Trent in a search for "persons in the water". Nothing was found and, soon after, the *Nottinghamshire* left for the long journey (not all of it under her own power!) to South Africa to which country she had been sold. Station records show that she went with the best wishes of Oban that, during her time in South African waters, she would be as dependable as she had been at Oban.

A total of 91 launches were made in the calendar year 1997, those not specifically mentioned above being in the "run of the mill" categories of machinery failure, divers or diving boats, medivacs and strandings.

Launches in 1998 created a record at Oban Lifeboat Station. Not only had it exceeded 100 launches for the first time but established an all-time record for the number of launches at a station where there was no inshore-lifeboat in addition to the all-weather boat – a remarkable statistic for a station established only in 1972.

It is ironic, however, that the first call of this particular year should turn out to be a hoax – a hoax that received massive press coverage as some readers may remember. At 0931 on 8 January 1998 Oban lifeboat was requested to join Islay, Campbeltown and Portrush lifeboats in the search for a 42-ft sailing boat, believed to be a catamaran, on passage from the west coast of Ireland to Preston, Lancashire. She had reported that she had one person on board and was unsure of her position, had no VHF radio (the distress call made by mobile phone) but had red flares. Oban Lifeboat was asked to conduct a radar and visual sweep towards the island of Colonsay after which she circumnavigated Colonsay before being stood down. She was refuelled and ready for service again at 1529 hours. We assume that, about then, the truth of the matter was emerging and it was understood that the lone sailor was subsequently charged by the police.

One of those services that brings tremendous satisfaction to a coxswain, his crew and the whole station took place on 10 January. As the crew and their guests were assembling for the annual dinner, Oban Coastguard reported that a canoeist was overdue at Cuil Bay, Duror, having set out earlier to do the short passage round the island of Balnagown. The lifeboat launched at 1912 hours and arrived on scene at 1952, first of all making a counter-clockwise search of the island followed by a mainland shore search northwards. As she was veering offshore to avoid the shallows at the mouth of the Sallachan Burn her searchlight picked up the canoeist clinging to the waterlogged canoe some 2 cables offshore with one arm wedged in it. Crewmember Dr Colin Wilson assessed the casualty's condition as being serious enough to have him airlifted by the rescue helicopter, also on scene, to hospital in Oban – meantime he was given oxygen on the lifeboat and made as warm as possible. The young man survived the ordeal but it would seem that the lifeboat found him just in the nick of time. At 2215, with the lifeboat refuelled and ready for service, the crew returned to the dinner.

Appendix II is a copy of a letter of thanks from the canoeist's father and which he is happy to have re-produced. On a technical point in this service, the Trent's autopilot proved invaluable when transferring the stretcher from lifeboat to helicopter – particularly as all the crew were engaged in securing the safety and welfare of the patient. On a non-technical point, the most worrying feature of the service for Jim Watson, the lifeboat's mechanic, was NOT anything to do with his two powerful 860 HP MAN engines but the fact that he had placed his favourite woolly hat on the casualty's head while waiting for the helicopter to lift him and was seen in the helicopter crew's video film grabbing the hat from the poor canoeist as he left the lifeboat – fortunately for Jim, that piece of the film was not shown in the next day's television news.

So much was learned during this service that it is worth repeating the report made by the coxswain a few days later. It forms Appendix I of this book.

Run-of-the-mill type services involving vessels broken down, vessels aground, medivacs and pregivacs continued thereafter. They included one in the annoying category of "needless" when, on 16 May, the coastguard sought the lifeboat's help in locating the source of a "carrier" signal on VHF channel 16. Such a signal, of course, blocks transmissions on this important distress channel and the lifeboat began the search. Puilldobhrainn, a popular anchorage just south of Oban, was being checked when the signal mysteriously ceased! Perhaps it was a child who had been playing with the radio or a handset whose pressel switch had fallen against an obstruction. Perish the thought that any sailor was responsible.

The long-awaited naming ceremony of the new Trent took place on 23 May 1998 at the South Pier when Mrs Lizanne McKerrell, wife of one of the trustees of Mora Edith Macdonald's estate, graciously named the boat. The day was grey and very windy and the platform party was hard put to prevent notes from disappearing amongst the seated guests numbering some 300.

The chairman of Oban Station, Willie Melville, opened the proceedings and lead the assembled company through the time-honoured and dignified ritual of a lifeboat naming ceremony. Mrs McKerrell was presented with a bouquet of flowers by young Rachel Henry, six-year-old daughter of Crewmember Ian Henry; Mr Guy Platten, divisional inspector of lifeboats, described the boat; Mr Lindley Carstairs, a trustee of the estate of the late Miss Mora Edith Macdonald, formally delivered the lifeboat to the Institution on behalf of all the donors; the boat was accepted by the late Mr Archie MacKenzie, DL, convener of the Scottish Lifeboat Council who handed her over into the care of Oban Station branch and accepted by Captain Norman MacLeod.

With the handover complete, Mrs Marie-Claire Williamson-MacDougall, president of the fundraising branch at Oban, made a humorous vote of thanks prior to a short ecumenical service of dedication, involving the Reverend Andy Campbell, Church of Scotland, Oban, the Reverend James Beaton, Free High Church, Oban and Father Roddy Johnston, St Columba's

RC Cathedral, Oban. The principal purpose of the ceremony was then achieved when Mrs McKerrell, in naming the boat, smashed a bottle of "bubbly" over the bows of the *Mora Edith MacDonald* and, with other guests, including the late Baroness Michie of Gallanach (then Mrs Ray Michie, MP for Argyll & Bute), was taken for a short sail in the new boat. Episode two of the day followed when all repaired to Oban High School for tea during which Mrs Mairi MacLeod, wife of the hon sec, cut a christening cake bearing a beautifully iced RNLI flag. Episode three (and the last one of the day) took place in the evening in Soroba House Hotel where mine host and a good friend of Oban Lifeboat, David Hutcheson and his wife, Edyth, not only laid on one of the superb meals which was the hallmark of Soroba House, but presented everyone with a quaich engraved "Mora Edith MacDonald, 23 May 1998" – a wonderful memento of the day and typical of the generosity of the Hutchesons, which had been present from the foundation of the station.

The only other-than-routine service in June was a launch to carry the local coastguard coast rescue team to a cliff on the island of Lismore where they had hoped to rescue a local crofter's sheepdog, which had fallen and was trapped. On arrival, however, the dog was in the final stages of being rescued by a member of the public who happened to be on the island and was a tree surgeon familiar with harnesses and cliffs.

On 9 July the lifeboat was launched to assist in the search for a rod fisherman who had fallen into the River Awe and was swept down-river to Loch Etive. Soon after launching, the lifeboat was advised that a body had been sighted on the east bank of the River Awe but was requested to continue to await confirmation that the body was no longer alive. Sadly this was found to be the case but the lifeboat remained at the river mouth until all of the rescue personnel were safely off the bank.

In the "lucky white heather" category on 6 August was a 32-ft yacht who had her mainsail blown out the previous day and now reported her engine had totally failed! The lifeboat met up with the casualty making little headway under spinnaker in the tidal race at Lismore Light. She was later secured by the lifeboat at Ardentrive.

On a medical evacuation from Mull a few days later, the patient, poor soul, was being sick pretty often with Dr Murchison asking Second Coxswain Douglas Craig to empty the sick bowl over the side periodically. On one occasion when the patient was given back the bowl, he asked, "Have you got my teeth, Doc?" The rest of the conversation is not on record.

One week later a young fish-farm worker severed his thumb in a feed-hopper and was taken aboard the lifeboat from a fish-farm workboat off Maiden Island for transfer to hospital in Oban. While transferring to the ambulance at the lifeboat berth, another workboat came alongside with the casualty's thumb in a box of ice. Ten years later the writer (who had delivered the thumb to the ambulance as it happens) was shown the hand and the perfectly re-attached thumb!

One of the less usual calls took place on 19 August when, after the discovery of unexploded ordnance (thought to be a WWII depth charge) near Maiden Island, the harbour was closed and the lifeboat patrolled the north entrance broadcasting warnings. She then escorted the MOD boat with the device to a safe area for disposal, which took place – at the second attempt!

On 28 August 1998 a middle-aged couple capsized a Mirror sailing dinghy in the area of the Torran Rocks, Ross of Mull, the lady successfully swimming ashore but losing sight of her husband. A full-scale search was undertaken involving Oban lifeboat, SAR helicopters from Prestwick and Stornoway and numerous vessels from the Ross of Mull and Iona. The search was suspended at 0130 hours and Tobermory lifeboat tasked to resume the search at first light. Regrettably, the missing man was not found.

Another launch with a sad result took place on 14 September when the lifeboat could do no more than bring the body of a diver back to the station for collection by the police. The diver had been inspecting his own yacht's mooring at Cardingmill

Bay, Oban when he got into difficulties and, despite attempts by ambulance crew and doctor, he could not be revived.

At the end of the day on 14 October nine men working on Eilean Muisdale at the south end of Lismore had reason to be grateful to Oban Lifeboat when, because of the sea state, the launch normally providing their transport to and from Oban was unable to collect them. The hon sec was asked if he could help and, after discussion with the coxswain, it was agreed to make an attempt to bring the men home. The lifeboat was launched at 1708 arriving on scene at 1723 and by 1736 had all nine aboard after Coxswain MacKechnie had made four approaches picking the men off in twos and threes. One might describe this as a "workmanlike" job.

On 19 October a small bulk carrier 76 m long ran aground on the west coast of the island of Kerrera. After obtaining permission as usual to attempt to tow her off, the lifeboat tried several times with no success, the vessel being firmly aground. No oil leakage was evident but her master suspected damage to Nos 2 and 3 double-bottom tanks and it was agreed to launch again later to assess the casualty's condition at low water. Two coastguard sector officers accompanied them and it was arranged to launch again for a third time to stand by if the tug *Anglian Prince* arrived in time to attempt a tow-off. When she did arrive and all things were considered, a decision was taken to delay the attempt until the following morning, the tug with surveyor aboard remaining on scene overnight. The final launch took place at 0435 hours to stand by the hoped-for refloating of the carrier. By 0607 the tug had succeeded in pulling the casualty clear and she made way to Oban Harbour under her own power and lifeboat escort.

Two thoughts spring to mind regarding this service – first of all, six of the seven lifeboatmen involved served on all four calls, turning out at 0705, 1221 and 1652 on the 19th and at 0435 on the 20th (and the seventh would have turned out if required) – remarkable dedication, particularly of the volunteers, and it must be remembered that many others were ready to fill any "vacancies". Secondly, it is a good example of how dependent the Institution is upon the ability and willingness of volunteer crew to drop what they are doing and dash for the boat and, in most cases, with the blessing (and pay) of their employers. Some who are self-employed may be the worst off especially if they are single-handed.

The 100th call of the year (and the record referred to earlier) was the evacuation of a patient with unstable angina from Mull.

The first call of the next 100 will not ever be forgotten, especially by the community of Iona and, more so, by some families on the island. At 0419 on the morning of 13 December, coastguard requested lifeboat assistance in the search for four young men in the Sound of Iona following the swamping and capsize of a 14-ft clinker-built dinghy, the alarm having been raised by a fifth man from the dinghy who had struggled ashore. Oban lifeboat, Coxswain MacKechnie in command, launched at 0430 while Tobermory and Islay lifeboats were also tasked to the scene as well as an RN helicopter from Prestwick and a CG helicopter from Stornoway. The upturned dinghy was found by shore searchers around 5am just south of Fionnphort and, shortly after, nearby, the body of one of the missing men, leaving three unaccounted for. The sole survivor, hospitalised in Oban, gave the Oban launching authority as much information as possible regarding the timing of the accident and the colour of clothing the others were wearing, all of which was passed to the searchers.

The five men were returning to the island of Iona from Fionnphort having been at a dance on Mull – a short passage with which all of them were extremely familiar. The dinghy had clearly succumbed to the stress of weather and all were thrown into the water. The first day's search was called off at darkness but resumed next morning, Oban lifeboat leaving Oban again at 7am and from 0900-1620, together with a helicopter, other small craft and shore searchers combed the Mull shore, Iona shores (all round the island), off-lying islets, rocks and skerries – sadly all to no avail. Conditions on both days were bad and searching in shallow water with a swell, demanded extreme concentration on the coxswain's part.

Most of the crew knew at least some of the young casualties and were under some mental stress as well. Their efforts were to be commended throughout a most testing service.

Other services making up the record year included some 13 medivacs from islands and vessels (including diving-related incidents), at least 10 calls to vessels aground or suffering engine failure and several false alarms with good intent. Those and others were dealt with routinely.

Calls in the year 1999 dropped slightly with a total of 87, these comprising three false alarms, 17 medivacs, 13 to divers or diving boats and the remainder a mixture of strandings, machinery failure and small boats in trouble along with another "policing" job at the southern entrance of the Sound of Kerrera while a bomb disposal team dealt with a WWII mine. Lifeboat crew were grateful, on several medical calls, to be accompanied by a paramedic or an ambulance man, especially when the crew list did not include a doctor member.

The date of the very first of the 1999 calls may give some clue as to the reason for it, taking place as it did on 7 January together with the fact that the man in the sea off the esplanade, to whom the lifeboat had been called, came ashore voluntarily into the hands of the police.

Another service spanning two days occurred on 13-14 January when an 18-ft dory, bound Salen, Mull from Lochaline with one man aboard, was reported overdue. In co-operation with several fishing boats, extensive searching of the area took place during which oars were found off Fuinary by one of the fishing vessels. The search was called off at 2300 hours and resumed at first light next morning covering much of the area searched the day before but also extending it to Bernera Island and the nearby Lismore shore. Sadly neither boat nor occupant was found that day although, six days later, the lifeboat assisted the police in the recovery of a body from the shore on the west side of the island of Lismore. No formal identification had been made but the clothing on the body reconciled with that of the missing man.

Another "overdue" incident, this one on 1 February, ended more happily when a lone sailor out of Lochaline and expected home by 6pm was found safe and well the following morning at 10.15 ashore at Inniemore Bay in the Sound of Mull. He had allowed his dinghy to float away when he landed the previous afternoon and, this being a wild, lonely stretch of coast with access only by sea or overland in rough terrain, he became stranded, spending the night in an old bothy there. The only "downside" to this service was that his non-return was not advised to coastguard until the following morning. Mobile phones were not as popular then as they are now but a brief call from this sailor to his home, had he had one with him, would have avoided the anxiety – and the lifeboat launch. This is NOT to say that "mobiles" should ever be thought alternatives to VHF transmitters – for example, a lifeboat often requests a casualty whose position is uncertain or unknown to broadcast on a given VHF channel so that her bearing may be established by the lifeboat's radio direction finding equipment. One of the several routine pregivacs deserving mention this year is the transfer on 27 June of a lady who was the sister-in-law of the first ever mother to give birth onboard in 1997. It had not become a family habit, however, as this member lasted out until she was in hospital in Oban.

On 8 August, 63 passengers aboard an Oban pleasure boat were probably quite glad to see the lifeboat appearing on the scene. Her engine had been misbehaving from time to time and had wisely requested the lifeboat to stand by as she headed for Oban Bay only some 1.5 miles away. However, her engine failed completely and the lifeboat towed her home. While just about to berth the casualty, the lifeboat received a call to go to the assistance of a small motor cruiser, with two persons aboard, drifting without power to the northwest of Port Ramsay, Lismore. A nearby charter angling vessel who had heard the call, offered to berth the first casualty for the lifeboat thus releasing her to head north to the latest problem – a typical example of the unwritten rule of the sea and of sailors. Arriving off Port Ramsay, the lifeboat found the motor-cruiser being held head-to-weather by a local charter boat from whom the lifeboat took over the tow and, because of sea conditions, proceeded into the lee of the island of Shuna before heading south, returning the casualty to her mooring in Loch Creran. Exactly one month later in a southerly 7/8 wind, the lifeboat responded to a call to launch to the assistance of a 26-ft whaler-type sailing boat with seven persons on board capsized in the Lynn of Lorn near Shuna Island. On reaching the scene the lifeboat found that six of the seven had been taken aboard their own rescue craft while the seventh, the skipper, was taken aboard the lifeboat from his liferaft. The lifeboat attempted, in vain, to take the capsized whaler in tow and returned to Oban where she landed the skipper having advised the coastguard of the co-ordinates of the waterlogged boat.

Launches in 2000 totalled 68 of which 21 were medivacs, divers or diving boats 15, strandings 11, the remaining 21 being the usual mixture of reasons. Those not detailed below were routine, divers being taken to the re-compression chamber at Dunstaffnage or to hospital while most strandings resulted in the casualty being towed off with no serious damage or water ingress.

On 29 January a French fisherman who had been landed on Mull by Tobermory lifeboat and was in Dunaros hospital, required further treatment/surgery in Oban. At this stage, the weather was such (WNW Force 6-7, gusting 8) that the sailing of the car-ferry *Isle of Mull* and her return to Oban was doubtful but, considering that it would be a much more comfortable journey for the injured fisherman on the larger vessel, the lifeboat launch was delayed until a decision on the ferry sailing was taken.

At her sailing time, however, she was unable to leave the berth at Oban and the lifeboat proceeded. The fisherman was landed to an ambulance at 1808 and transferred to hospital.

A patient being brought to Oban Hospital from Mull with heart problems in February had an unexpected detour via the marina at Craobh Haven. Shortly after casting off at Craignure, Mull the lifeboat was tasked to a vessel having a fire on board and arrangements were in hand to have the patient landed at either Easdale or Cuan slips and transferred by ambulance to Oban from there. The patient, however, insisted on remaining on the lifeboat which headed for Craobh Haven with fire pump and hoses rigged, only to find the casualty had made port on one engine where fire engines were in attendance. The human casualty made hospital in Oban soon thereafter.

The only mayday call of the year was from a yacht with five persons on board which had struck a reef in Loch Craignish in June. While under way to the casualty the lifeboat was advised that all five had been picked up by young lads with a dinghy but one or more had been in the water and Crewmember Dr Colin Wilson was landed to assess the condition of the party while the lifeboat laid out a kedge anchor from the casualty, which was still partially afloat – this with the assistance of a crewman from a nearby yacht. Of the survivors, one was taken to hospital for treatment if necessary.

A medivac which was not the usual "milk-run" to Craignure was carried out in June – this one to the east side of Loch Craignish, which is accessible only by boat. A 14-year-old on a Duke of Edinburgh Award expedition had suffered leg injuries in a fall and was brought aboard the lifeboat on the "Y" boat (small inflatable carried for such purposes) and transferred to an ambulance waiting at Ardfern.

A medivac somewhat more serious than many occurred on 30 July 2000 when a lady who had had an accident while on a quad-bike was brought to the mainland from Mull, suffering from a broken tibia and fibia and severe facial injuries. Dr Murchison, fortunately, was on board.

A 37-week pregnant lady in labour was evacuated from Mull on 1 August and the crew was again relieved to have the presence of Dr Murchison on board. The lady, however, held out and was transferred to hospital in Oban before the arrival of the baby!

A larger number of persons than average were taken aboard the lifeboat on 5 August at 1500 when a vessel carrying 12 divers and three crew ran aground at Rubha Garbh Aird, near Ardmucknish Bay and was taking water. Two lifeboat crewmembers and a pump were put aboard the casualty but, after the pump had been running for ten minutes, the water level had not receded and the lifeboat returned to station for a second pump. All the divers were taken aboard the lifeboat and landed at Dunstaffnage, the two pumps now just coping with the ingress of water, which appeared to be through the sheer strake. At 1900, Second Coxswain Craig, in command, estimated that a further 1 ft of tide was necessary to refloat the vessel and established a tow-line at 1930. The casualty was refloated within a few minutes but, with her engine unable to pump cooling water, was towed to Oban and berthed there.

Another of the unsuccessful launches to divers/diving vessels occurred on 21 August when a faint mayday call was picked up by Oban Coastguard at 1102 from such a boat. The lifeboat launched at 1106 and soon learned that a male diver, now aboard his mothership, had surfaced rapidly from 62 m and was not breathing while his female companion was missing. A very intensive and extensive search, covering an area of some 25 nautical square miles, got under way involving an SAR helicopter, fishing vessels, RIBs and yachts but without finding the diver – a sad end indeed as the male diver also died.

The policy of having the lifeboat escort a "recovered" casualty for a time, after repairs or re-floating, paid off on 24 August when a single-handed 26-ft yacht in the area of Fladda Light reported engine failure and the lifeboat was launched to assist. When under way to the scene the lifeboat was advised that the yacht had managed to re-start her engine. In view of darkness falling and the single-handed situation, the lifeboat decided to escort the casualty to Craobh Haven. It soon became apparent that she was disabled again when she stopped and no radio calls were being answered resulting in the lifeboat towing her into Craobh Haven.

Local knowledge is unbeatable when close-quarter manoeuvring is required and every opportunity is taken by the coxswain to familiarise himself and his crew with, particularly, any features which may have changed or caused to be changed within his "patch". For example, on 13 September, when the service to an overdue diver in Loch Creran was called off as the diver had turned up and was adamant in his refusal to have the lifeboat doctor check him over, the lifeboat, almost at the new road bridge over the loch, took the opportunity to check the depths etc around the bridge supports – not altogether a fruitless shout.

It is often the case that visitors to the west coast of Scotland, with perhaps only minimal sailing experience, feel that when they go afloat in sea lochs well away from the OPEN sea, they will be "OK". In November two occupants of an 18-ft boat which they had trailed from home found themselves in difficulty in Loch Etive – their engine had failed and they had no idea where they were. The lifeboat located the casualty with husband, wife and son aboard, took husband and wife aboard the lifeboat and put a crewmember aboard the small boat to assist the son. She then towed the casualty to Taynuilt pier to await being put on a trailer. If this service demonstrates anything it is that, despite being in sight of land virtually all round and well inland from "the sea", difficulties can arise regarding position – and, of course, engine failure can occur anywhere.

A WNW wind of Force 7 turned what might have been the fairly simple recovery of a fish-farm RIB into a reasonably difficult as well as lengthy task, involving as it did, the fish-farm barge, the fish-farm RIB and the fish-farm steel boarding boat. On 19 November, a small fish-farm RIB went ashore on the west side of Lismore due to broken steering and stranding one man ashore while another was still on the fish cage. Second Coxswain David Graham put one crewmember aboard the RIB to assist and another on the fish cage to help secure the RIB and, with one fish-farm worker, boarded the small metal boat on a nearby mooring, this being the workers' means of getting ashore at their base in Craignure, Isle of Mull from their main boat. A heavy swell throughout made the whole operation very difficult and in view of this, the weather generally and the inexperience of one of the men, the lifeboat escorted the fish-farm vessel, with her boarding boat towed astern, to Craignure.

Launches in 2001 totalled 77 – comprising 18 medivacs, 10 strandings, seven to divers and divers' boats, seven to machinery failures with the balance made up of persons in the water, vessels unsure of their position, man overboard services, and the usual few false alarms with good intent. One of the most effective and rewarding services took place within 30 m of the lifeboat berth on 16 April when a man was reported to be in the water between two fishing boats (crabbers) moored alongside the South Pier. The wind was 7-8 from the NNW making that corner of the bay very rough and confused. When Crewmember Ronnie MacKillop, kitted in a dry suit, entered the water and swam to the fisherman, he found him in a lifebuoy and secured by a rope round his upper arm. This rope was held by a second fisherman who obviously also had been in the sea and Ronnie MacKillop began swimming the unconscious, but still breathing, man to the lifeboat. This was extremely difficult, with waves breaking over both Ronnie and the fisherman, an additional fear being that the unconscious man would fall out of the lifebelt. Lifeboat Second Mechanic Keith Burnett, also in a dry suit, then entered the water and their combined efforts succeeded in landing the casualty on the lifeboat at her waist. The other fisherman, suffering from hypothermia, was also taken ashore by the lifeboat and both men taken to hospital by ambulance.

This was a difficult service in which the co-operation between lifeboat crew and police probably saved one life, if not two. Great credit is due to Second Coxswain David Graham, in command that night, for keeping the lifeboat at a safe distance from the fishing boat in the strong north-northwesterly wind while the unconscious man was being taken aboard and also due to Crewmembers Ronnie MacKillop (now coxswain) and Keith Burnett for their work in the water. Apart from the crew aboard the lifeboat, three other members assisted ashore. For this service Ronnie received a framed letter of thanks from the Institution.

Although mobile phones should never be used as alternatives to marine VHF radios they can be useful at certain times. In July, a small sailing dinghy capsized in Seil Sound. Why didn't the two-man crew simply right her and sail on as is normal in dinghy-sailing? Because she had turned 180 degrees and fouled her mast on the bottom! The two men had little alternative but to sit on the upturned hull from where they used a surprisingly still-dry mobile phone to call the coastguard! By the time the lifeboat reached the scene the men had been taken off by a RIB from a Customs Cutter and were then transferred to the lifeboat. Lifeboat Crewmember Ronnie MacKillop donned a dry suit and succeeded in righting the dinghy, which was then taken in tow by the lifeboat to Balvicar Boatyard along with her crew who, despite having spent almost two hours on the upturned hull, were cold but not hypothermic.

It's another girl! The second birth aboard (see 5.8.97 for first) was on 13 September 2001 when Kerrie Hazel MacGillivray made her entry to this world at 06.16 hours as the lifeboat entered Oban Bay.

Midwife Hazel Munro joined the crew on this service (much to the relief of the lads who were without Crewmember Dr Colin Wilson on this occasion) and it was not surprising to find that the new baby's middle name is Hazel! The return of service shows the hon sec's remarks as "…Coxswain and crew suffering from a mixture of elation and shock…all recovered after a bacon roll and a mug of strong tea". *(Aye, right! – author.)*

On 5 October 2001 Oban Lifeboat, for the first time in many years, operated north and west of the Sound of Mull. The shout was to assist a 14-m yacht with engine failure and an exhausted crew somewhere between the Isle of Coll and the northwest entrance to the Sound of Mull. Why? Well, Tobermory Lifeboat was on restricted service (the description given when a lifeboat, usually for some technical fault, is not able to operate at 100%) and Mallaig Lifeboat, having launched to the casualty, had to return to station when a crewmember suffered a heart attack. Oban lifeboat, departing at 0555, reached the casualty two hours 22 minutes later, took her in tow and secured her on a mooring in Tobermory two hours 27 minutes later. After the Tobermory crew had revived the Oban contingent with tea and rolls, they headed for home and were ready for service again at 1335 hours – all in the day's work!

The rock north of Innis Island claimed yet another victim on 24 October 2001 when a large powerboat with three persons on board struck it and made water immediately. Despite the lifeboat putting a pump aboard and operating it for over two hours, the rising tide won and pumping had to be abandoned, personnel and pump being taken back aboard the lifeboat.

Launches totalled 62 in the year 2002 including 12 medivacs, eight machinery failure, six divers/diving boats, five strandings and four false alarms.

The first service of the new year, on 14 January, followed the finding of a bloodstained nightdress on the shore at North Ballachulish whereupon a full-scale search was commenced for a possible missing person with everyone fearing the worst. Nobody had been reported missing or overdue, however, and later it was discovered that, on the previous evening, a girl's nightdress had been used in the rescue of an injured duck! It was never established whether the owner of the nightdress had been wearing it at the time it was pressed into service as a bandage.

Seven people were glad to see the Trent on 2 April when they sat in a waterlogged RIB off Lismore after seas had swamped the boat, "killing" the engine. The wind was southeasterly Force 5 with accompanying swell. The lifeboat towed the casualty to Puffin Dive Centre, Oban taking six persons aboard leaving one to man the RIB – all were landed safely ashore.

The two youths seen running from the slipway at Portbeag, Oban on 10 April just as a car was seen running into the sea off the slip have probably no real idea of the outcome of their crime, their stupidity and their foolishness – they were never caught. The first report of a car entering the sea (without further information) inevitably suggests that there may be a person or persons in the vehicle. This has to be assumed until found otherwise and, accordingly, considerable stress is put upon coastguards when requesting the lifeboat launches, upon the lifeboat hon sec and crew when getting to the station as quickly as possible and upon the coxswain and crew when on scene. Neither must the poor owner of the car be forgotten – hopefully, he or she will have insured the car but the trauma cannot be to their benefit, especially if old-aged. In this case no one died or was injured but it certainly did the car no good.

On 8 June 2002 a diver sustained severe lacerations to a thigh and had the wounds dressed by two lifeboat crewmembers to prevent further loss of blood. Fortunately, the lifeboat was already at sea on exercise and the patient was in an ambulance to hospital within 30 minutes of the lifeboat's arrival.

If a yachtsman falls to the deck from the mast, it is better not to be from the tall mast of a former America's Cup contender. The unfortunate crewman on *Sovereign* suffered severe lacerations to both legs, torn muscles and ligaments, which were attended by the ambulance crew before taking him to hospital.

The launch on 30 July to transfer a crewmember with a dislocated shoulder from a yacht in the marina at Kerrera, half a mile away, ought to have been a short service but, in the event, took one hour 23 minutes all told. First of all the yacht from which the injured man had to be evacuated was the middle one in a trot of seven boats and the individual concerned was found to be inebriated, making the transfer a slow business. Then, on the way back across the bay to the waiting ambulance, two youths in a small dinghy were spotted and appeared to be not exactly comfortable in it so, after transferring the patient to the ambulance, the lifeboat returned to investigate. The youths were drunk and disorientated, the dinghy was believed to have been stolen so youths and boat were brought ashore – possibly avoiding a bad situation becoming worse.

On 29 September a diver suffering from de-compression sickness picked up by Mallaig lifeboat was transferred to Oban lifeboat when the two boats met in the Sound of Mull. Within 40 minutes the diver was ready for treatment at the re-compression chamber in Dunstaffnage.

When the station HMA and crewmember, Dr Colin Wilson, was not available for a variety of reasons and the expected injuries to be dealt with were maybe a bit beyond the first-aiders on the crew, the station had the ready and superb assistance of the local ambulance station. On 31 October 2002 the ambulance paramedic, Donald Morrison, joined the crew and dealt professionally with a crewmember of a small fishing vessel whose hand had been caught in the winch wire, dragging it over the pulley. The injured man was landed to an ambulance at Ellenabeich.

The ready co-operation between lifeboat stations was again in evidence on 6 November 2002 when a fleet diving tender, having been refloated by Oban lifeboat in the Sound of Mull after a grounding, was escorted to Tobermory by Tobermory lifeboat.

The remaining launches of the year were dealt with in an almost "routine" way, involving mainly straightforward jobs. In truth, no coxswain ever treats any launch as "routine" although some allow the adrenalin to pump at lower speeds than others.

The year 2002 ended on a tragic note when, on Hogmanay, a small 7.5 m fishing vessel with two persons aboard was reported overdue, the lifeboat launching at 19.14 hours. A search of the Firth of Lorne was conducted and, at 22.12, the Search and Rescue helicopter reported a semi-submerged vessel about halfway between Oban and Lismore Light. The search was suspended at 0210 and resumed at 0800 next morning when a briefing of all rescue personnel was held at Oban Police Station. The lifeboat first of all landed police teams of mountain rescue members and Coastguard coast rescue teams on the Creag Islands then commenced further sea searches within pre-determined co-ordinates covering the area concerned together with the Customs Cutter, the SAR helicopter and several fishing boats including *Enterprise, Kyrene, Porpoise* and *Odyssey*. By noon, the teams on the Creag Islands had completed their searches with no result. Neither was anything found at sea and the search ended at 1515 hours – a tragic outcome at any time but more so for the families concerned at such a time of the year. On a few occasions in the next few weeks the lifeboat chose to carry out her regular exercises within the search area but to no avail.

Three days later on, 4 January 2003, the first medical evacuation of the year took place on the "doorstep" as it were. A crewmember of a large fishing vessel berthed at the South Pier sustained a severe head injury while in the hold of the vessel and the most practical means of transferring him to an ambulance was to take him aboard the lifeboat alongside the fishing boat and take him to the ambulance from the lifeboat slip.

When investigating a report of a mine west of the Garvellochs on 31 January 2003 the Royal Navy inflatable craft tasked with the job was operating near her upper limits and Oban lifeboat escorted her from Easdale to the search area. After concentrated searching nothing was found and the lifeboat escorted the RN craft back to Easdale before returning to Oban.

Of the remaining 55 launches that year, 18 were medical evacuations from islands or vessels, four were due to mechanical failure, five were false alarms with good intent, eight were to strandings and 20 to a mixture of swamping, fouled propeller, capsize, adverse conditions and those where others had coped before the lifeboat's arrival.

A small 3-m inflatable with outboard and six persons aboard in a northeasterly Force 5 on passage from Eilean Dubh off Lismore to the mainland is not the happiest of scenarios. Shortly after the party left the island, the dinghy, not surprisingly, was swamped and wisely returned to the island while the engine still had life in it. Not many, if any, small inflatables carry VHF radios but, again, the good old mobile phone came to the rescue, the party calling the coastguard by using it. The lifeboat was launched within six minutes of being requested, arrived on scene 17 minutes later, took all six persons aboard, set up a tow and landed all at Oban 46 minutes later still. In the month of April spending the night on an uninhabited island with no water is not something to relish.

One of the benefits of the larger lifeboat and, therefore, larger crew is that, at times, the coxswain is able to spare one, and perhaps two, of his crew to board a casualty to give assistance – cutting the 4-man Brede crew by half would seldom have been possible. On 18 June, however, the Trent was able to loan two men to assist an elderly lady sailing a 9-m yacht single-handed when she found herself in difficulty in a southerly wind of Force 6-7 and poor visibility in the Firth of Lorne. The yacht was escorted safely into Oban Bay.

On 17 July it surely looked like a "David & Goliath" situation when the Trent went alongside a 68,000 ton American merchant vessel in the Firth of Lorne to evacuate a lady suffering from a broken femur. Ambulance man John Barbour joined the crew for this service, monitored the casualty's condition and accompanied her to hospital in the ambulance.

A truly "AA"-type job was done on 19 July when the lifeboat was launched to the assistance of a 12-m yacht making water in the Sound of Mull. It transpired that the cause of the ingress of water was due to a shaft seal becoming loose, this established by a lifeboat crewmember who re-fitted it and the yacht continued on her passage escorted by the lifeboat for a mile or so to confirm that the repair had been successful. Within six minutes of returning to the station, she was launched again to rendezvous with Tobermory lifeboat off Loch Aline and transfer a "bent" diver to the re-compression chamber in Dunstaffnage. No sooner had the diver been landed than the Trent was off on the third service of the day to a grounded 6-m motorboat on Eilean Dubh Beag with a failed engine. On arrival, the casualty was found to have re-floated and was taken in tow to Oban, the two occupants coming aboard the lifeboat.

One launch of a lifeboat can be to the novice sailor while the next may be to the most experienced. Successive services to each of these categories took place on 28 July and 1 August respectively when, first, an inexperienced crew of three in a 10-m yacht in the Firth of Lorne radioed for assistance in establishing their position. The lifeboat located them at midnight, put a crewmember aboard to assist their passage into Dunstaffnage and was back on station ready for service again at 0204 hours. Secondly, three days later, two experienced sailors at the end of a transatlantic passage, also in a 10-m yacht, requested assistance to enter Oban Bay, their propeller being fouled. There was no difficulty in towing them into Ardentrive Marina where it was learned that they had been unfortunate enough to pick up a section of fish-net somewhere in the ocean – no great difficulty in the open sea when sailing but a different story when in confined waters trying to come alongside a pontoon. Oban Lifeboat was pleased to be able to help in both cases.

If one has to fall 7 ft from a bunk on to a stone floor and land on one's head, it is better not to do it in one of the remotest spots in the north-east of the island of Jura. This fate, however, befell one poor soul who had his injury dressed and monitored on board the lifeboat by ambulance paramedic Donald Morrison while en route to hospital in Oban.

One of the launches of the type that leave lifeboat crews dissatisfied occurred on 26 August. A seemingly genuine 999 call reported a female voice "shouting and screaming" in a small dory-type boat in the Sound of Luing area. Conditions were excellent – weather dry, visibility very good, wind nil, sea state glassy calm – all perfect for searching and the lifeboat launched at 2150. A radar search of the Sound was conducted first of all and found nothing then engines were stopped but nothing broke the silence. An illuminating parachute flare was sent up and a message sent via the deck speakers still without result. Adjacent islands' shores were searched until the coxswain was satisfied that no craft was in difficulty and the lifeboat returned to Oban and was ready for service again at 0152 hours.

On 14 September 2003 excellent co-operation between a rescue helicopter and lifeboat saw a very elderly lady, who had suffered a stroke on board the sailing ship *Jean de la Lune*, airlifted to hospital in Oban. The rigging of the large ship prevented the helicopter from winching the patient from the deck so she was taken aboard the lifeboat and landed ashore at an old pier from where the helicopter winched her up and off to Oban!

Calls dropped somewhat to 44 in 2004, comprising medivacs from vessels or islands – 11, strandings – 3, machinery failure – 9, false alarms with good intent – 4, dragging anchors – 2, others coped – 10, miscellaneous – 5.

The year got off to a sad start on 29 January with the drowning of a member of the two-man crew of *Multicat* engaged in fish-farm work who had entered the water to swim after the boat, which had drifted away from the feed barge leaving his companion stranded there with no means of communication. The alarm was raised only when *Multicat* was found ashore in Ardmucknish Bay with engine running, navigation lights on but nobody on board. The lifeboat continued the search together with other vessels and a Search and Rescue helicopter until 0125 hours when all were stood down, the search resuming at first light next day. After some two hours of searching the following morning one of the fishing boats involved reported having found a body whose clothing carried the name of the missing person.

Before the month was out, the lifeboat was launched to investigate the report from a member of the public that he thought a yacht was in trouble off the tidal "gate" known as the Dorus Mhor at the entrance to Loch Crinan/Loch Craignish. The *Mora Edith Macdonald* left Oban at 1750 and, just under an hour later, commenced the search round Reisa-an-Sruith then eastwards through the Dorus Mhor, round Garbh Reisa and Eilean-na-Cille. She then headed westwards to search Kinuachdrachd and round into Bagh Gleann nam Much in the Corriebhreacan before covering the south shore of Scarba and up the east shore to Rubha Fiola. Nothing was found but the first informant was perfectly in order in reporting the possibility – the thought that anyone might be in trouble in these nasty tidal waters, albeit not particularly windy waters that January night, had to be investigated.

Despite the fact that lifeboats are sometimes at sea when conditions are atrocious and that, even in good weather, they are called upon to operate in shallow and/or rocky areas, they sustain relatively little damage. All coxswains are obliged to report ANY damage, however slight, while they are at sea and it is to their great credit that such reports are minimal. A typical example of this occurred during a service to a vessel aground in the Sound of Luing on 21 February during which the casualty's skipper requested a line from the lifeboat in order to keep his stern off the shore in the strong tide. Rocket-propelled speedlines from the lifeboat were unable to be secured by the casualty's crew and the coxswain had to close the casualty to establish a tow but, in doing so, briefly touched the bottom at low speed slightly damaging a side keel – a small price for the recovery of the casualty who was escorted to Oban and secured alongside the North Pier at 0535 hours.

On 15 March a suspected engine room fire on a fishing vessel saw the lifeboat tow the casualty into Oban but, before escorting her to her own berth, allowed her to land her catch at the fish pier – priorities are always established correctly in the West Highlands!

A Norwegian yacht of some 13 m was seen to ground twice on entering Oban Bay just before midnight on 28 March 2004 and was guided in by the lifeboat to the railway pier. Of course, she ought to have carried local charts or at least the Clyde Cruising Club sailing directions but, were the position to be reversed and a sailor from the UK to find himself feeling his way into a small Norwegian harbour at that time of night, it would be re-assuring to have a helping hand from the locals.

There being no vehicular access to the Boy Scout camp site at Barnacarry Bay on the southern shore of the entrance to Loch Feochan, the young man who suffered an injured shoulder had to be evacuated by lifeboat to hospital in Oban. An ambulance crew had made their way to the campsite and assisted in the transfer of the patient to the lifeboat, the patient being accompanied by two interpreters since he had no English.

The occasional shout is eventually laughable – especially when it is found to be in the "mistaken" category – such was the case on 26 September when the lifeboat was launched to the assistance of four persons standing on the upturned hull of a vessel in Loch Etive. Shortly after launching the lifeboat was recalled, it having been established that the capsized vessel was an upturned catamaran specifically used as a platform for angling.

On 30 September 2004, the lifeboat with a fairly crowded wheelhouse left Oban for Mull. Apart from the lifeboat crew there were 11 members of Oban Mountain Rescue Team on their way to search for a missing person on the island of Iona. Iona's highest point is only 99 m so the word "overkill" comes to mind! However, a holidaymaker had apparently "disappeared" leaving her belongings in her lodgings and the search for her was on. In addition to coastguard coast rescue personnel, the mountain rescue team was brought in to assist but the search discontinued when the "missing" person called to say that she was "OK" and hadn't bothered to take home all of her belongings!

A 76-m merchant vessel with engine failure required lifeboat assistance in a SE Force 7 on 14 December to prevent her from being blown ashore on Insh Island. The lifeboat duly answered the call and arrived on scene in good time to pass a tow – there the problem arose. It took some considerable time to indicate to the non-English-speaking crew of the casualty that the tow rope should be made fast and not thrown back to the lifeboat! The tow was eventually established and course set for Oban. After half an hour the merchant ship managed to re-start her engine and continued to Oban under lifeboat escort with a lifeboat crewmember aboard to act as pilot for the entry to Oban Bay.

CHAPTER VIII

2005-2008

The year 2005 saw a total of 61 launches comprising 22 medivacs, seven strandings, six false alarms, nine machinery failures, nine others coped and eight miscellaneous. With regard to the "false alarm" heading, it is worth noting that these launches are only categorised <u>after</u> the event and some may be lengthy searches at the end of which the lost or overdue person is found never to have been lost or overdue.

When a mobile telephone <u>would</u> have come in handy was on 6 July when a canoeist was reported as overdue from a trip in the Camus Ridire area of the Sound of Mull. A canoe and some clothing was found by the lifeboat on the shore at Inniemore Bay leading her to search the shore up to Ardtornish Point and around the nearby islands. This found nothing and the lifeboat arranged to pick up seven coastguard coast rescue members from Craignure returning to further comb the Morvern shore. About 9pm the missing man was found safe and well – presumably having lost track of time or perhaps having forgotten when he had stated he would be home! The lifeboat was ready for service in Oban again four hours after she launched.

On 7 July the inspector's exercise did not require to be "staged" since, when setting out with inspector on board, coastguard requested the lifeboat to divert to a 40-ft Belgian yacht with machinery failure. One lifeboat crewman was put aboard the casualty and reported that the propeller shaft had sheared at the gear-box coupling! This provided the inspector with an excellent opportunity to check all aspects of the coxswain's approach to a live shout – locating the casualty, identifying the problem, setting up an efficient tow and securing her alongside in Oban.

Near gale force winds on 24 August 2005 resulted in three boats getting into difficulties in Puilldobhrainn anchorage about 0300 hours when, first of all, one yacht dragged anchor and snagged the anchor of a second nearby yacht. When on scene the lifeboat put two crewmen aboard the first boat which, by now, had found she also had a fouled propeller. The tangled anchors were lifted and both vessels assisted to re-anchor, the first still with a fouled propeller. By 0520 hours a third vessel, a motor-sailor, had also been driven ashore, was making water and required immediate help. The lifeboat pump was put aboard and, once re-floated, tow to Oban commenced. The lifeboat, knowing that she had still to return to assist the first boat, was extremely grateful to the FV *Spaven Mhor* who offered to take over the tow, releasing the lifeboat to return to the casualty and take her in tow to Ardentrive, Kerrera.

A service in the "exceptional" category took place just after noon on 17 September 2005 when the *Mora Edith Macdonald* was launched to the aid of the 12-m yacht *Classic Wave* reported to have lost power off the south-west corner of the island of Kerrera. Because of road works in Oban town centre, crewmembers answering the pagers were held up and the coxswain wisely decided to proceed with a crew of five (one short of the usual complement), the yacht now reported to have grounded and was making water.

On the short run to the scene, the salvage pump was prepared for use and Coxswain Ronnie MacKillop made an initial pass to assess the situation. He found that the casualty was on a shelf of rock with large areas of kelp to starboard and astern. A small area of deep water lay to port. A swell of about 2-2.5 m was made worse by the backwash from the rocky shore behind the yacht and the southwest wind was estimated by the coxswain now to be around 30 knots.

Asking the yacht's crew to recover a floating tow-line, which a fishing vessel standing by to assist had cast off at the lifeboat's suggestion, Ronnie then took the lifeboat alongside the casualty's port quarter where Crewmember Peter MacKinnon, third mechanic, climbed aboard with the salvage pump and set it in motion. Soon, however, it became apparent that, because of the damage to the hull and the incoming tide, the pump was not coping and a decision taken to abandon ship, at which point Ronnie took the lifeboat back alongside to take off the four men. Only one of the yacht's crew was able to scramble aboard the lifeboat as the two vessels rose and fell in the swell of over 2 m and the coxswain took the decision to launch the lifeboat's own liferaft and manoeuvred the lifeboat, stern to the casualty's stern, where the remaining two yachtsmen and Peter had gathered to await the lifeboat's liferaft. Peter then remembers a shout from the lifeboat "There's a rope round your leg" but before he could free it *Classic Wave* slipped off the rock shelf and sank immediately. The two yachtsmen managed to grab the liferaft and were blown away from the wreckage into deep water where the lifeboat picked them up. Peter, however, was dragged down with the yacht but with incredible strength found from somewhere he clawed his way back to the surface where he held on to *Classic Wave's* mizzen-mast still showing above the surface. It was as if a prayer had been answered for, just then, the yacht's own liferaft popped to the surface right beside him. The exhausted Peter managed to hold on to it as it, too, was swept away into deeper water where the lifeboat recovered him – a thankful conclusion for a man who had, several times, had the opportunity to get back aboard safely himself during this incident but chose not to. On return to Oban the three yachtsmen were examined by paramedics in the ambulance and needed no further medical attention while Peter was taken to hospital but released later. Both Ronnie and Peter received framed letters of thanks for their efforts that day. (A medal would have been more appropriate – the author.)

"It's yet another girl!" The third birth on board (see August 1997 and September 2001) took place on 6 October 2005 when baby Emma Cato was born during the passage from Craignure, Isle of Mull to Oban. When in future poor Emma has to state her place of birth, strictly speaking she ought to answer "56°26.04N 5°32.08W" but probably "Oban" will be acceptable. Perusal of these three dates of birth would suggest that the next might be in November 2009 – it may be a boy next time!

With medical evacuations from islands and vessels showing a drop, calls in 2006 totalled 52 – 16 medivacs, eight machinery failure, eight diving incidents, the remaining causes being strandings, dragging anchors, capsizes and fouled propellers.

By the end of January, Oban has usually recovered from the excesses of the New Year celebrations – except perhaps for the odd individual. It may or may not have been an extension of these which led to the police seeking lifeboat assistance in February to land a handcuffed gentleman and four police officers at the lifeboat slip from a fishing vessel, it having been found impossible to land directly ashore due to the height of the tide. Lifeboat authorities were pleased to help.

In April the lifeboat's intervention "bought time" as it were, when a vessel carrying supplies of fish feed got into difficulties in the Firth of Lorne and the skipper managed to beach her just prior to her engine failing. The lifeboat put two crewmembers with two pumps aboard the casualty and the water level was able to be controlled while the fish farm's own work vessel unloaded the cargo. This not only saved the cargo but assisted greatly in re-floating the casualty which the same boat towed to Corpach for repair. One lifeboat pump was left aboard for the passage to Corpach and returned next day.

Before the month was out the lifeboat attended a party of divers in three boats in a rough sea. One of the boats had capsized leaving three divers in the water who were pulled aboard the second boat but it was found impossible to right the capsized vessel.

The lifeboat took five persons aboard from the second boat, which was now overloaded (the third being already "full"), and asked her to secure the lifeboat's tow-line to the "upside-down" vessel. The capsized boat's bow shackle could accommodate only a small rope and the lifeboat's veering line had to be used, resulting in the tow parting four times during the fairly slow passage to the dive centre where all personnel and boats were returned safely.

Five days later the *Mora Edith MacDonald* was tasked to investigate a fishing vessel in the Firth of Lorne seen to be constantly circling with no sign of anyone aboard. The lifeboat manoeuvred alongside the mystery vessel and put a crewmember aboard who reported that there was a crewman in the wheelhouse – sound asleep!

On 20 June the Easdale Island ferry reported a yacht "in difficulty" in Easdale Sound where she was found to be anchored in rocky shallows with an ebb tide and a forecast of severe weather imminent. The casualty had no power and no communications and the lifeboat's XP boat landed two crewmen aboard her to assist. Thereafter the XP boat held the yacht in position while her crew made sail, the lifeboat escorting her to Oban where she was taken alongside and moored at Oban Yacht Services.

In July, 20 passengers on a trip to Mull aboard one of Oban's several pleasure boats that cater for tourists enjoyed some excitement at no extra cost when their boat suffered engine failure and grounded on rocks near Duart. The lifeboat towed the casualty off the rocks and back to Oban with all 22 tourists and two crew still aboard.

That Coxswain MacKillop's home is only a few yards from the Sound of Kerrera resulted in a fast launch on 6 August. Ronnie had just gone to bed when he heard what he described as "a high-speed impact" on the water near his house. Reporting the incident to the coastguard he then activated the pagers and the lifeboat was launched immediately. Once on scene a large rigid inflatable was found on Heather Island, 10 ft out of the water and above the high-water mark. Two people were aboard and were, incredibly, not seriously injured – one only having a small cut on the nose. The XP boat was inflated and sent ashore to bring the two persons to the lifeboat, which then landed them at the lifeboat slip – where they were met by the police.

A 999 call to Clyde Coastguard on 24 August saw the *Mora Edith MacDonald* heading for Kinlochleven to search for a person in the water. Coastguard, however, became a bit suspicious as a result of the caller's behaviour and because some of his statements did not "ring true" – so the call (from a mobile) was checked upon. Surprise, surprise – coastguard enquiries revealed that this was the tenth hoax call from that number on that day – and, wait for it – the 79th hoax call from the same number since July!

Towards the end of August, coastguard requested lifeboat assistance in tracing an EPIRB "hit" but, once at sea, only a very weak signal was picked up somewhere to the south and the lifeboat headed in that direction. The search area was narrowed down to Ardfern Yacht Centre where Islay Lifeboat, also on the search, joined in and, using both boats, it was confirmed that the EPIRB was ashore there. A coastguard team searching ashore was asked by a member of the public what they were looking for and, on hearing the answer, confessed that his wife had put an old EPIRB in one of the boatyard skips earlier in the day! The coastguard team then asked the lifeboat to wake the lady and take her ashore to identify which skip the beacon was in and it was duly recovered! It is likely that the weak signal was because of the beacon's position in a steel bin.

Launches in 2007 totalled 48 comprising the usual mixture of medivacs, strandings, overdue vessels etc including the following:

The first shout of the year was to another possible EPIRB "hit". On 6 January, Clyde Coastguard requested that Oban lifeboat be put on immediate readiness as they awaited the next "pass" of the satellite. At 1130 hours the lifeboat was requested to go to a position some seven miles west-north-west of Oban while monitoring 121.5 on the way. Tobermory Lifeboat was also asked to assist but shortly after both lifeboats were stood down, coastguard having received further information and were satisfied that no one was in danger.

At the end of January a large fishing vessel whose draft was too great to allow her alongside in Oban required to land an injured crewman to hospital and the lifeboat met her in deep water well down the Sound of Kerrera where the casualty was taken aboard and transferred to an ambulance at Port Beag.

On 16 April a fishing boat reported finding two persons in the water in the area of the Gulf of Corryvreckan but it was not known whether further persons were involved. The lifeboat was asked to continue searching while the two casualties were being taken ashore where, at Craobh Haven, they were conveyed to hospital in Oban by Rescue Helicopter 177 – sadly only one survived. When coastguard were able to confirm that no other persons were unaccounted for, the lifeboat continued to search for the missing canoe for some time without success before returning to station.

On 24 June if <u>any</u> vessel required lifeboat assistance it was the 30-ft yacht that had blown out her head-sail, whose mainsheet track had failed and who was single-handed! Two lifeboat crewmen were landed on the casualty to help the skipper stow his flogging sails and set up a tow – this to Oban Marina where he was left on a mooring.

The only fact that differentiated the shout to the "bent" diver on 9 August from the many other similar services was the fact that he was 77 years of age! He was taken from Mull to the Dunstaffnage re-compression chamber from where it is understood he made a good recovery.

On the same day, returning from a call, the lifeboat received a radio request from a yacht that was probably in sight and, therefore, knew she was at sea, requesting assistance in lowering their jammed mainsail. Two lifeboat crewmen went aboard the casualty where they winched the skipper up his mast to clear the problem.

How to treat a canoeist IN his canoe suffering from a dislocated shoulder after capsizing can be something of a problem – he certainly can't do much to help himself. On this occasion, the coxswain asked his accompanying friends to tow him ashore and despatched two crewmembers in the XP boat to render first-aid ON the beach before taking him to the lifeboat in the XP boat. He was then transferred by ambulance to Oban hospital.

The *Mora Edith MacDonald* was again involved in medical duties when, in August, she was launched to embark a sick member of the crew of a large sail training ship some 10 miles south-west of Oban. The sea was fairly choppy so the training vessel lowered her sails and motored at about 3 knots with the wind on her port side providing a lee to starboard for the lifeboat. After discussion between the lifeboat doctor and the doctor aboard the sail training vessel, it was agreed to transfer the patient to Oban hospital using the lifeboat.

A "stand-by" job brought August to an end when a large general cargo ship lost power some 12 miles south-west of Oban. The casualty being in open sea, there was no need to establish a tow and the lifeboat merely stood by while attempts were made by the ship's engineers to correct the problem. However, at 2330 hours she drifted over a shallow bank where she promptly dropped anchor. The lifeboat was stood down and returned to station. The cargo ship managed to restart her engine about 0500 hours and resumed her passage.

There is nothing nicer after a hard day's sailing than to anchor or pick up a mooring, wash and change then head ashore for a pint at the pub. The crew of one yacht did just that on 16 September, going ashore at 2000 hours but on returning to the yacht at 0100 hours things didn't go according to plan – the yacht had gone! The coastguard, on hearing the news, took the view that the vessel adrift was a danger to shipping and requested the lifeboat to launch and try to locate the boat. The search was successful, the missing boat being found high and dry at the north end of the island of Lismore. It is likely that a commercial salvage arrangement would have been made to recover the vessel.

It is thought that a television programme highlighting the island of Lismore had inspired a mother and her son to visit the island one Sunday in November. They had parked their car on the mainland at Port Appin, crossed on the ferry and walked the length of the island on the only road, intending to return by what they thought a more scenic route off the road. A reasonable idea, but darkness defeated them and a 999 call resulted in the lifeboat being diverted from her passage back to the station from an abortive shout and tasked to attempt to find them.

From the description the lady gave it appeared that they were somewhere in the south-west corner of the island and the lifeboat proceeded to that area requesting that she activated the flash on her camera when she saw the boat. She did so, her position was pinpointed and the XP boat was launched to bring them out to the lifeboat, which returned a much relieved mother and son to Port Appin.

Two thousand and eight saw the slowest start to a year ever! It was 8 February before the pagers were activated other than for the weekly test. This originated with a fishing boat, berthed alongside the breast wall leading to the North Pier, having fallen over at low water but failing to re-float with the flood. The coastguard team attending the incident then became concerned for the safety of one crewman who had not appeared and requested lifeboat assistance. Once on scene and unable to get alongside for lack of water, the coxswain launched the XP boat to assess the situation, the outcome being that no-one could reach the shore since the vessel had fallen away from the wall and was now surrounded by deepening water. The lifeboat stood by until it was clear that all was well.

Of the other 15 launches during the first half of the year, three were to diving incidents (usually bends or suspected bends), three in the "others coped" category, four routine medivacs from Mull, one medivac from the island of Lismore, one medivac from a vessel, one engine break-down in tidal waters but no wind, two in the "FAWGI" bracket.

When a member of the public saw a small rowing boat with one person in it, fishing on Loch Creran in April 2008, and about one hour later saw the same boat still floating on the loch but, this time with nobody aboard, he dialled 999 and the lifeboat was launched. While the lifeboat carried out a search, the coastguard coast team made enquiries ashore and identified one individual who had been fishing earlier and had come ashore, failing to secure the boat, which had floated off on the tide!

In the same month, a second shout in the "FAWGI" category took place when a farmer on the island of Kerrera reported what she thought was a vessel sinking west of the island. Once on scene, the lifeboat found a large piece of fish farm equipment which, from a distance, the coxswain said did indeed look like a boat half-submerged – the farmer confirmed this was the object she had seen and it was retrieved shortly after.

When a man walking on a remote part of the island of Lismore with his wife on 13 May 2008 fell and injured his leg, his wife left him to fetch help. The island nurse attended and wisely requested lifeboat assistance, it being much easier for the patient to be put in the lifeboat's small XP boat and taken out to the lifeboat and thence to Oban, than to be taken across rough terrain to the only road on the island before an ambulance could pick him up.

In June 2008 the evacuation from one vessel involved a little more than just taking a patient aboard the lifeboat. The skipper of a yacht had injured a hand badly while working with the anchor and required medical treatment fairly urgently but his crew were not experienced enough to sail the boat to a safe anchorage. Two lifeboat crewmembers were landed on the yacht to sail her back to Oban and the skipper was driven to Oban hospital by local coastguard who met the lifeboat.

A 16-m yacht with her anchor fouled on the bottom in Ardentrive Bay, Kerrera began to yaw wildly consequently putting the other vessels around her in danger of being damaged. Her crew were unable to cast off the chain and required lifeboat assistance. Two lifeboat crew were put aboard the casualty while another was landed on the nearest moored yacht with a large fender. The anchor chain on board was eventually freed, buoyed and cast off for attention later.

A few days later on 9 August a mayday call was made by two kayakers, one of whom was in the water, requesting help in a rough sea, heavy swell and strong tide. They gave their position as The Grey Dogs, the passage between Scarba and Lunga, and both SAR helicopter from Prestwick and Oban lifeboat proceeded. The charter vessel *Porpoise* (who had relayed the original mayday) and the fishing boat *Golden West* both reported that they could find nothing in The Grey Dogs but some 25 minutes later the coastguard received a mobile telephone call from the canoeists saying that they had made shore safely but didn't know where they were. The helicopter ultimately spotted them at the east end of the Corriebhreacan, about 3 miles from their assumed position. The lifeboat then picked up the men and returned them to Loch Melfort.

On two occasions during a week of bad weather towards the end of August, the Scottish Air Ambulance was unable to fly due to weather conditions and the lifeboat carried out the evacuations.

CONCLUSION
A line under the services recounted in this story has to be drawn somewhere and the writer has drawn it at the end of 2008. No doubt, during the time it will take to edit it and have it published, Oban lifeboat will have launched many more times but, perhaps, someone will take up where he has left off and keep the history of this splendid station up to date.

CHAPTER IX

FUND-RAISING

As is mentioned elsewhere in this story, the RNLI is self-supporting and fund-raising is of enormous importance to its continued existence. Since the Institution is now 184 years old, one might say that fund-raising has been fairly successful – by far the greatest proportion of income still emanating from legacies.

Legacy income alone, of course, leaves an enormous shortfall in the annual figure required to meet outgoings and fund-raising committees throughout the length and breadth of the land work tirelessly to raise the necessary finance. Only a few years ago was the name of those committees altered to "fund-raising" from the well-known "Ladies Lifeboat Guild" – this reflecting the very welcome entry of menfolk to the cause of raising finance.

In Oban, the ladies' guild already in existence received a real fillip in 1972 with the arrival of a lifeboat of their very own – the natural result of seeing, daily, on her mooring, the tangible lifeboat representing a cause which they had been supporting for many years.

Little did the writer of this booklet know when, as a teller in the Garelochhead sub-branch of the National Bank of Scotland (now Royal Bank) in the late 1950s, when cashing the monthly pension cheque of Angus Cameron, the retired manager of the Oban branch, that there was an RNLI connection. Only when researching the history of Oban Ladies' Lifeboat Guild, more than 50 years later, did it surface. Angus Cameron had called a few local ladies together to raise funds for the lifeboat Service sometime in the early 1930s thereby "founding" the first lifeboat fund-raising committee in Oban. One of its members was the Lady Provost, Mrs Christine MacAllister, an aunt of Miss Isobel Black, a name that was to be synonymous with lifeboat fund-raising in later years.

The name of Isobel Black later became prominent in all of its work – her home-made marmalade and second-hand book sales are, to this day, still playing a part! It is not surprising, therefore, that Isobel has been the recipient of four awards from the Institution, viz, a gold badge, a bar to the gold badge, a statuette and a certificate of thanks. The other ladies to have been awarded a gold badge are the late Mrs J MacPherson who was also a recipient of the Queen's Jubilee medal in 1977 and Mrs MC Williamson-MacDougall, much better known as just "Marie-Claire". The enthusiasm, arm-twisting and work carried out by Marie-Claire are all legend – in particular, her sales of Gallanach (her home) daffodils to shops, banks and offices will long be remembered.

These individuals are, of course, only representative of countless ladies (and now gentlemen) who organise soup kitchens, coffee mornings, quizzes, flag days, book fairs, jumble sales, fashions shows, a flower festival, talent competition, a thrift shop, film shows and miscellaneous other events. Silver and bronze badges, statuettes and certificates of thanks have also been awarded to many others too numerous to mention.

One event which the lifeboat crew organised on behalf of the fund-raising committee was the Great Oban Raft Race in 1981 which became an annual race until 1995 raising many thousands of pounds over the 15 years of its being. It was possible in these days to combine the raft race with an exercise involving an RAF Sea King helicopter from Lossiemouth which not only provided coxswain and crew with valuable experience for the "real thing" but presented a spectacle for the public surrounding the bay and, hopefully, filling the lifeboat collecting cans. Gone are these days but it is gratifying that at least two pilots or winch operators still maintain contact with the station.

Taking its place as the principal source of fund-raising in Oban came a joint venture between Oban Lifeboat Station and Oban Distillery. Oban Distillery staff, under the leadership of their manager Ian Williams, had been enthusiastic participants in every Lifeboat raft race held – on one occasion entering two teams – and, when these races lost appeal, Ian Williams floated an idea across the lifeboat's bows for a replacement. He suggested to a meeting of the lifeboat crew that it might just be possible to stage a fund-raising event in the distillery – and, quoting from Mr Williams' report of that meeting, "…after a moment's silence the look of bewilderment on the faces of the crew gave way to smiles of anticipation as ideas for displays and fund-raising events began to flood forth." So was "Malt 'n Salt" born – a combination of the whisky industry and the Lifeboat Service – and was to be the station's largest fund-raising event for the next five years, the first taking place in July 1996.

The week before saw all sorts of lifeboat equipment being delivered to the distillery and after close of production on the Friday the distillery was hoaching with lifeboatmen putting things up, taking things down, suggesting this, suggesting that and, with distillery staff help, generally trying to create order out of chaos. Slowly the distillery became a living exhibition of the Lifeboat Service. The distillery staff had, for many weeks, been appealing to their various suppliers for prizes for the lucky straw draw and for several other attractions which they had thought up. The "icing on the cake" was when United Distillers announced that, not only would the day's takings for distillery tours be donated to the RNLI, but that all the money raised by distillery staff would be doubled under the company's fund-raising scheme. A busy day ended with a barbecue thoroughly enjoyed by lifeboat and distillery personnel and, all in all, the scene was set for a repeat the following year.

In 1997 the event was extended to include the Sunday afternoon and to embrace a whisky-nosing competition and a first-aid demonstration – both of these by a volunteer team of helpers from United Distillers, Elgin. One of the most popular attractions was the idea of model-maker Marshall MacKinnon of Edinburgh who brought up his fleet of radio-controlled lifeboats to be sailed at £1 a "go" by aspiring coxswains in a large pool constructed in the distillery yard. Both lads <u>and</u> dads enjoyed it!

To quote the distillery manager again, the lifeboat/distillery connection formed "a unique partnership". In addition to the Malt 'n Salt events, the distillery marked the arrival of the Trent-class lifeboat in June 1997 when the "retiring" Brede and she met bow-to-bow, allowing Ian Williams to welcome the Trent with a generous splash over *Mora Edith Macdonald's* bows of Oban 14-year-old West Highland single malt. As he said himself, "What remained in the bottle was put to good use ashore in the celebrations which followed!" The Trent's arrival was further marked by the distillery when they presented the station with a suitably inscribed quaich, the symbol of The Classic Malts. This quaich remains on display in the lifeboat station with, hanging nearby, an inscribed whisky cask-end commemorating the donation of a hogshead of Oban malt whisky to the station in 1994 in celebration of the distillery's bi-centenary. The cask is laid down in the warehouse at Oban Distillery to mature until 2012 when it will be removed and the contents bottled for use – the sale proceeds going to RNLI funds – altogether a wonderful and generous donation.

Before leaving the fundraising field, the substantial annual income during West Highland Yachting Week deserves specific mention. After the race to Oban, which really opens the week, Oban lifeboat "meandered" amongst the fleet, holding out a bucket for contributions – and, particularly on sunny days, those sailors sitting in their cockpits discussing the race and perhaps having the odd libation, dug very deep in their pockets. Oban Lifeboat thanks them very much – more especially since, in recent years, they have been "got at" also by Tobermory Lifeboat!

CHAPTER X

NORMAN MACLEOD
AND JOHN PATRICK MACLEAN

The writer makes no apology for singling out these two gentlemen for special mention. One of the most important factors to which the success of the foundation of Oban Lifeboat Station must be attributed was the virtually simultaneous appointments of Captain Norman MacLeod as honorary secretary and John Patrick Maclean as coxswain/mechanic. Both men had been professional seamen in the Merchant Navy, both had "swallowed the anchor" and both were now working in Oban, Norman as a teacher of navigation (later principal teacher) and Patrick in his jointly-owned motor repair garage. Norman is the son of a seagoing father, Calum MacLeod from the Isle of Berneray where Norman spent his first few years from the age of six weeks having been born at his mother's home of Strontian. Pat Maclean also has Gaelic roots being the son of John Maclean, former rector of Oban High School and a member of the well-known Maclean family of the island of Raasay.

Both are possessed of keen minds and calm, thoughtful dispositions. This, together with their seagoing backgrounds and experience, ensured that a group of extremely enthusiastic individuals, most of whom were amateur sailors, were turned into a cohesive crew able to do what was required in the more serious circumstances they were to find themselves in.

Some 36 years on, it is not surprising, therefore, that both are the proud holders of the MBE, Patrick being awarded his in the Queen's Birthday Honours list 1997 and Norman, his, in the Queen's Birthday Honours list in June 2002. Needless to say, both awards were in recognition of the tremendous work each did in the interests of the RNLI, each of them for in excess of 20 years.

CHAPTER XI

VISITORS TO THE STATION,
THE LIFEBOAT AND THESE WATERS

Royal Yacht *Britannia*

It is a sad fact that British governments are prone to "miss the obvious" in respect of what raises the profile of the United Kingdom and one of the worst was the decision to take the royal yacht *Britannia* out of commission. No other country in the world produced such a platform for their Head of State, who deserves no less. Instead of replacing the vessel with an up-to-date version (no doubt costing much less than the Iraq war expenditure), they chose to deprive Queen and Country of this great asset. She is now, more or less, a museum piece – albeit an interesting one.

For many years HM The Queen travelled to Balmoral, for her annual holiday there, on board *Britannia* and for most of these voyages the royal yacht sailed north through the Sound of Mull passing Duart Castle, home of Lord Maclean, close friend of the Queen and Lord Lieutenant of Argyll. There, the royal yacht and Duart Castle exchanged a few spectacular displays of pyrotechnics and Oban Lifeboat, at an appropriate time and with the Lord Lieutenant's permission, paid respects to Her Majesty by making a run past *Britannia* dipping her ensign, which was acknowledged appropriately by the royal yacht. This took place for many years, the most memorable being the evening when *Britannia* requested that the lifeboat delay her pass by 20 minutes. The lifeboat duly complied – to be "rewarded" when two figures, one of them unmistakably Her Majesty, appeared on deck and waved enthusiastically to the lifeboat. It was a dreich evening and they were the only persons to be seen – it is thought that the other was the Princess Royal, herself often a sailor in these waters. The crew of those days remember these occasions with pride – sadly they are no longer possible.

HRH The Duke of Kent's Visit

The highlight of 1980, shore-side, was the visit to the station by the president of the RNLI, HRH the Duke of Kent on 4 June when, accompanied by Sir Charles McGrigor, convenor of the Scottish Lifeboat Council and Colonel RMT Campbell-Preston, DL, he met coxswain and crew, the Ladies' Guild members and other officials of the station before inspecting the lifeboat and having tea in the "Shed"! Security checks in advance of such a royal visit, as one can imagine, are thorough and widespread and, indeed, so they were during the week leading up to the visit. No one, however, can recall a large barrel of bait (which many may remember sitting at the head of the slip for weeks – and really odiferous) being checked as to its contents!

HM The Queen's Visit

In 1995 Her Majesty, accompanied by the Duke of Edinburgh, visited Oban in very much better weather than previously in August 1956 when rain and high winds were the order of the day, forcing her to re-join *Britannia* from a launch which she had to board over a few fish boxes in the relatively sheltered Sound of Kerrera.

On 8 August 1995 Her Majesty opened Lorn and Islands District General Hospital and later in the morning met several local personalities including Coxswain Patrick Maclean and his wife, Liz, at a gathering in the Argyllshire Gathering Hall. Later in the day on the North Pier, the lifeboat crew were introduced to the Queen and the Duke by the hon sec, Captain Norman MacLeod. Both had something pertinent to say to each of the lads, the Duke appearing to be quite keen to go afloat on the lifeboat – something not on the agenda that day! The lifeboat did, however, escort the royal barge returning Her

Majesty and the royal party to *Britannia* at anchor just outside Oban Bay.

Having mentioned royalty it is time for boasting of the others who have been very welcome visitors to Oban lifeboat or station. It is inevitable that one or more will be omitted and the writer takes full responsibility for any such errors – and apologises now.

The first VIP (other than RNLI "brass") to visit the station was the late Very Reverend Dr David Steel while he was moderator of the General Assembly of the Church of Scotland. His visit took place on 26 July 1974 when, accompanied by the late Reverend John MacLeod, minister of Kilmore and Oban Parish Church, he was taken to sea in the ILB for a brief trip – wearing the moderatorial shoes with the silver buckles!

Other well-known names who were welcome visitors to the station include Dame Judi Dench, that lovely, homely lady and talented actress with her equally talented husband, the late Michael Williams, a charming, modest gentleman with their delightful daughter, Finty. The fine singer, Kenneth MacKellar and chairman of the Scottish Tourist Board, Alan Deveraux also visited the station. The outstanding actor and lifeboat supporter, Robbie Coltrane, visited the station and went to sea in the lifeboat when generously giving his time and talents in making the Sunday evening BBC appeal for a charity – on this occasion for the RNLI.

The latest personality to become a welcome visitor to Oban Lifeboat is Sir Jimmy Savile. Jimmy has not only just paid a couple of visits to the station, he "sang for his supper" on both occasions. These events were the station open days in 2005 and 2007 when he not only officially declared the day "open" but remained amongst the stalls for the rest of the day, chatting with virtually everyone in sight and readily posing for photographs at any time. There are not many personalities who, after officially opening fetes, etc, do not take their leave of the function fairly soon thereafter and the success of those two open days was in no small way down to Sir Jimmy's continued presence – he has, not surprisingly, been made an honorary crew member of Oban Lifeboat.

The late Archie MacKenzie, vice lord lieutenant and the late Sir Charles Edward McGrigor, BT.

No history of Oban Lifeboat Station would be complete without reference to the above two gentlemen. Archie MacKenzie, another of Nature's gentlemen, was always a welcome visitor to the station whether on official RNLI business or merely calling in because he happened to be in Oban. Archie was, of course, steeped in the ethos of the RNLI and held the post of convenor of the Scottish Lifeboat Council for several years and, in that capacity, attended the naming ceremony of the *Mora Edith Macdonald*.

Sir Charles, a predecessor of Archie MacKenzie in the post of Scottish convenor, was another great friend of the station. Sir Charles, or Eddie as he was known to many, always considered Oban Lifeboat Station as his "local", living as he did on Loch Awe side. He and Lady Mary were often visitors to the station and his influence on the successful outcome of the new berth, referred to under "The Mutiny", will always be appreciated. On his death in October 2007, his coffin, lead by a piper, was borne from church to graveside by retired members of Oban Lifeboat crew and Mike Vlasto, chief of operations.

CHAPTER XII

UNUSUAL LAUNCHES, AWARDS, OUTSIDE EVENTS ETC

"VITAL"

The keeping of a radio log is a statutory requirement in all vessels and is particularly important in a lifeboat where the contents of some logs may have to be reproduced in a court of enquiry. The maintenance of a radio log is a difficult, sometimes impossible, task, especially on a lifeboat moving at speed in a seaway and, accordingly, logs were often "cobbled" together using the notes which the launching authority had made from the radio exchanges he managed to pick up on the station radio, notes scribbled on the lifeboat itself, coastguard radio logs and recollections of anyone else involved.

This was a far from satisfactory situation lacking the accuracy necessary for production in a court of law and, for some time Coxswain Pat Maclean and Crewmember/Medical Adviser Gordon Murchison had been considering a solution. In 1990 these two men suddenly made the breakthrough – they conceived what, with hindsight, was a blindingly simple answer – using a standard cassette tape recorder. All incoming and outgoing messages on the lifeboat would be captured on one track of a stereo tape while the second track would carry a speaking clock of the type used by the blind. Assistant Lifeboat Mechanic Malcolm Robertson, a marine electronics engineer, was brought into the frame and soon had constructed a prototype which worked perfectly and was used on Oban lifeboat for several years thereafter.

The acronym "VITAL" was coined by Dr Eleanor Wilson, wife of Crewmember Colin Wilson, when she named it "Voice Initiated Timed Automated Log".

One extremely valuable by-product of the device, which the inventors had not initially recognised, was the ability of the hon sec or deputy launching authority to write up the service by simply taking the tape from the lifeboat's machine and retrieving, in the station or his own home, not only the accurately-timed facts but also the "flavour" of the shout reflected in the voices of the crew, coastguard or casualties.

The invention was nominated in the "innovations" category of the annual Silk Cut Nautical Awards by a member of the RNLI Committee of Management, Dr Bill Guild and was runner-up. As lifeboat speeds increased, reinforcing the need for an alternative to a written radio log, the Institution approached a specialist company in secure communications systems to evaluate two prototypes in 1993 (one being the Oban version) and, today, all lifeboats carry some type of voice recording system – Gordon, Pat and Malcolm's input was not altogether in vain. It is sad to report that Gordon and Malcolm are no longer with us, Malcolm having died in October 2004 while Gordon passed away in March 2008. Patients of Gordon as a GP/anaesthetist and customers of Malcolm (particularly fishermen) lost two of the most willing and able practitioners in their respective fields who would travel many miles at any time of night or day to help where they were needed. Malcolm's RNLI flag-draped coffin was borne from the church by his lifeboat colleagues while Gordon's ashes were scattered from the lifeboat in the Firth of Lorne by his son and daughter, Kyle and Gail. It almost goes without saying that their families' loss and grief was matched by Oban Lifeboat Station and their colleagues there.

Silk Cut 'n' Sail Boat-building Competition

In 1990 for the second successive year, Second Coxswain Douglas Craig and Crew-member Alasdair Maclean (now deputy second coxswain) reached the final stages of this competition held at the Southampton Boat Show. The competition challenges entrants to design a boat that can be built in less than seven hours using a limited supply of materials and tools and which can survive, and possibly win, just one race, in the Solent, including a leg in which only sail must be used. Coxswain Pat Maclean designed the boat, which they named *Taking Silk*, the team hoping to equal their previous year's success when they won a special prize for "the most elegant craft", coming ahead of professional yacht designers including Ian Nicholson of AA Mylne. This category was created only because of the standard of the Craig/Maclean entry!

Animal in the Water

Further confirming that the saving of life in lifeboat terms is not confined to human life, one service in 1976 ably demonstrated it. In October a Cal Mac ship was disembarking cattle at Oban for the annual sales at Corson's Mart when a frisky beast kicked over the flakes and jumped into the bay. When the launching authority was called it was to say that a Mart stockman was hanging on to the beast from a vertical dockside ladder and could the lifeboat assist?! The MacLachlan ILB launched immediately and took the heifer (for that's what she was) alongside the boat and headed for the nearby slip, relieving the stockman from his perilous post.

The beast, however, facing forward, was struggling to keep her head above water so she was turned to face aft and was successfully landed on the slip whereupon she tried to jump in again! She was restrained, however, and was returned to the Mart – from where the lifeboat's good warp was recovered next morning!

Stretcher Exercise

Exercises can often be repetitive, uninteresting affairs – with the odd exception. Following the theory that a casualty thought to be hypothermic ought not to be taken from the water vertically lest the sudden release of the hydrostatic pressure causes a fall in blood pressure known as post-immersion collapse with dire consequences, the station honorary medical advisor organised an exercise in January 1984. This involved one crewmember, who was feigning unconsciousness in the water, being pushed into a basket stretcher by another and having the stretcher hoisted, maintaining the casualty in a horizontal position by the use of ropes at head and foot. Unfortunately, the man on the head-rope got out of step with his counterpart on the foot-rope, the stretcher assumed a 45 degree angle and the poor "casualty" shot into the water as off a chute. As if this wasn't bad enough, when he surfaced he was met with the sight of the crew lined up on the deck, each declaring "5.6 for style", "5.1 for technical merit" and so on!

The Annual National Service for Seafarers

In 1905, the centenary of the death of Horatio, Lord Nelson, a British shipmaster, Captain R Hubbard, suggested to the nation in letters to the Press, that this year would be a fitting occasion in which to inaugurate an annual service in St Paul's Cathedral, not only to commemorate Nelson, but to remember all seafarers in whatever capacity they serve. This proposal was enthusiastically supported and in October 1905 the first such service was held and, with the exception of WWII years, has been held ever since. For the last 30 years the cathedral has been filled to capacity, the congregation occasionally including members of the royal family.

The colours of several organisations closely connected with the sea are paraded every year and have always included that of the RNLI. In 1989, the Institution allocated the duty to Oban Lifeboat Station and the three crewmembers (colour bearer and two escorts) who were honoured to represent the RNLI, would never forget the experience. They, of course, wore the kilt and the first of a few funny moments during the run-up to the event took place when the lassie in HQ at Poole, on hearing that the kilt would be the dress-of-the-day, asked "will the kilts be matching?"!! A short explanation to her followed – including the fact that even although two of the three had the same surname, all three tartans would be different. The colour-bearer was Willie Melville and the escorts, Mike Robertson and the late Malcolm Robertson.

Two crewmembers had never had any marching experience and the third, who <u>had</u>, undertook to take them through the basics by drilling them, parade-square style, in a large garage owned by the Royal Bank and which was more or less empty in the evenings. All went well until one evening a bank customer, who garaged his car there, came in unexpectedly to find these characters marching, slow-marching, halting, about-turning and carrying out miscellaneous other military steps – it will never be known whether or not he believed the explanation he was given.

On 10 October 1989, the colour party of three, accompanied by their wives, joined the Fort William –London "sleeper" at Tyndrum Upper Station and, despite falling out with the sleeping-car attendant, arrived safely at King's Cross next morning. A rehearsal at St Paul's took place that afternoon during which a chief petty officer, RN marched all seven colour parties up and down the main aisle from the west door to the High Altar countless number of times. Seemingly satisfied, he dismissed our three heroes (and the others) until the start of the service. Outside on the cathedral steps, still with the colour, the three kilted lifeboatmen were surrounded by tourists (mainly Japanese) wishing to have their photographs taken with them.

At 1800 hours precisely all seven colours entered the cathedral and were marched to the High Altar to be laid there for the duration of the service as the capacity congregation sang the hymn *Praise to the Holiest in the Height* to the accompaniment of the band of Her Majesty's Royal Marines. It was something that nobody present could not have found moving – certainly the Oban Lifeboat party and their wives will remember it for the rest of their days. A moving service followed, the solemnity of the occasion only being broken when one of "our" three opened his sporran to take out his handkerchief and out with it came a pandrop (probably last Sunday's) which appeared to hover for a moment before falling and "skittering", for ever it seemed, across the tiled floor! The RNLI colour is a beautiful work of art in silk. In 1984, the RNLI's 160th anniversary, The Clothmakers' Foundation generously sponsored an official ceremonial colour for the Institution commissioning the Royal School of Needlework to undertake the work. The colour was presented to The Queen Mother, a patron of the Institution, at the 1984 annual presentation of awards in the Festival Hall, London when she handed it over into the care of that day's colour-bearer, Coxswain Leonard Patten of Newhaven.

The Balloon

Early on a Sunday morning the lifeboat was launched to the assistance of a fishing boat perilously stranded on rocks a few miles south of Oban. As the coxswain assessed how best to approach the vessel to take off her crew, he saw a small red float on his starboard hand and mentally noted to avoid it on the run-in. Some time later, once the fishing boat's crew had been safely evacuated and, indeed, the vessel refloated by the lifeboat, the small red "float" was picked up and turned out to be balloon sold in aid of Cancer Research and to which was attached a label bearing the words "Elaine Mulgrew", an address in Lanarkshire and "please write". A letter was duly sent to Elaine telling her where her balloon had been found and asking her, in return, to let them know where she had released it! Elaine did more than that – with her mum and dad and little brother she paid a visit to the station where she met the coxswain and crew and told them she had released the balloon at Kirkfieldbank in Lanarkshire – over 70 miles away, as the crow (or balloon) flies. The Mulgrew family were given a conducted tour of the lifeboat and Elaine had her photograph taken on board – all because one of the country's best known charities picked up a balloon released in aid of another!

Clachan Bridge – Bicentenary – 1992

When the world-famous Bridge-over-the-Atlantic (linking the mainland with the island of Seil) reached its 200th birthday in 1992, great celebrations were held around the bridge and, not being too far from station, Oban Lifeboat took part. Only children were allowed aboard and, when the coxswain was able to see through the throng on the foredeck, he took the boat under the bridge a short way to the utter delight of the youngsters. As he did so, Oban Pipe Band played stirring tunes on the bridge above.

What's Going On?!

In late September 1997, skippers of ferries and fishing boats alike were puzzled when they saw Oban lifeboat steering the craziest of courses at varying speeds in the vicinity of Sgeir Donn just west of Kerrera – there seeming to be no apparent reason for the vessel's behaviour.

All was made clear, however, when it was revealed that the well-known reporter Alan MacKay, then with BBC's *Reporting Scotland* team, had been filming the lifeboat in connection with his forthcoming report on the embezzlement of charity funds in Glasgow, a figure of around £30,000, which had been destined for the RNLI. Alan and his camera crew had been positioned on the rock, Sgeir Donn, while the lifeboat made several passes in all directions close by.

The following week, the "set" was again in the Sgeir Donn area while a new publicity film was made for the RNLI, part of the commentary for which was narrated by former Beirut hostage, John McCarthy, himself a keen yachtsman. During the previous six years following his release from captivity, he made a fascinating film for television with Sandi Toksvig in which they sailed from the Channel Islands to the Orkneys and which many people still remember.

Ship's Bells

As we go to press, three bells are in the course of being engraved, each with the name of one of the three babies born aboard since the station opened. Oban Lifeboat crew decided to adopt and adapt a custom originating in the Royal Navy whereby a baby could be baptized under the ship's bell or using the bell filled with water for the ceremony and thereafter inscribing the child's name inside the bell. Since none of the three children born on Oban lifeboat (so far!) was baptized on board, the decision was taken by the crew to inscribe each bell and present it to the "baby" when he or she reached the age of 18.

Wedding Bells

Another first! On 25 November 2006 Crewmember Finlo Cottier married his fiancée, Liz Cook, in the lifeboat station. In a moving ceremony the pair exchanged vows and, in the company of relatives and friends, including lifeboat colleagues, they were lead by a piper in walking from the station to the nearby Manor House Hotel to celebrate the marriage.

Hans Frederik Gude

What does the Norwegian romantic artist, Hans Gude, have to do with Oban Lifeboat Station? The connection is fairly tenuous but the story is worth telling. Around 1990, the late Sir Charles McGrigor (see previous mentions) brought in to the station a postcard size print of a painting by Gude which hangs in the National Gallery of Norway in Oslo. Sir Charles had received this from a friend who had been visiting Oslo and who had recognised that the artist had painted the oil, or certainly the original sketches, from almost exactly the site of the present station and thought Oban Lifeboat personnel might be interested.

They certainly were and contact was made with their colleagues in the Norwegian lifeboat service to ascertain whether it was possible to obtain a copy of the original from the gallery. Using the crew fund, the copy was purchased but not posted to Oban – instead, one of the Norwegian lifeboatmen, coming to the UK on business, brought it to Oban where, at a small ceremony in the station, the hand-over took place and gifts were exchanged. Earlier in the day, the "messenger" was taken for a short trip in the Brede and, thereafter, given a tour of Oban Distillery by the manager, Ian Williams.

What had not been appreciated was that it measured 4 ft x 2 ft 8 in and considerably more when framed – in short, no wall in the station could do it justice and, after much photographing of it by the crew, it was presented to David and Edyth Hutcheson of Soroba House Hotel who gave it pride of place in their dining room. The crew felt that this, in some small way, recognised the immense input to Oban Lifeboat by the Hutchesons over many years. The station was delighted to learn that the painting did not go with the hotel on its sale years later but went with Edyth and David into their retirement home in the North.

Every picture Tells a Story

The photograph of the Watson *Dorothy and Philip Constant* on her mooring in the south-east corner of Oban Bay was the reason for the station being provided with a 12-ft inflatable dinghy to replace the 9-ft version the crew had used from the outset to board the lifeboat. Some reluctance on the part of the then inspector to make a larger dinghy available subsided immediately when it was pointed out to him that this picture was of the boat ON her mooring and not under way as he had thought. The photograph shows clearly, of course, that the rudder is in the "up" position confirming it all! Even with the larger boat, boarding and coming back ashore in fresh northwesterly winds was sometimes quite difficult.

Yet Another Picture

As has already been said, the naming ceremony of the *Mora Edith Macdonald* was attended by Mr Lindley Carstairs, one of Miss Macdonald's executors to whom the station presented a painting by local artist Bob MacCulloch. The painting was of the *Mora Edith Macdonald* and carried a brief caption explaining its background. Many years later Mr Ranald Mackay, a well-known West Highland yachtsman, saw the painting in an Edinburgh art shop window for sale, recognised the subject, read the caption and discovered it had been put up for sale following Mr Carstairs' death.

Mr Mackay promptly bought the painting at no small cost and presented it to Oban Lifeboat Station where it now hangs – a generous and thoughtful gift.

CHAPTER XIII

RECENT INITIATIVES BY THE INSTITUTION AS A WHOLE

Over the past ten years or so, several innovations have been introduced in fields hitherto not on the RNLI's agenda. Although not all directly affect Oban Lifeboat, they are extremely important in achieving the Institution's purpose as a whole.

RNLI beach lifeguards now cover 70 beaches in the UK. It could be said that this is a move in an attempt to reduce the launches of ILBs – a wise one at that, the lifeguard highly likely to be "on scene" beside the person in difficulty before an inshore lifeboat could reach him or her. The combination of both, however, is a splendid step forward.

In the late 1990s the Institution set up a new programme entitled "SEA Check" (Sea Equipment Advisory Check) which might be summed up as "prevention rather than cure". By 2000 the programme was really getting into gear with the employment of ten co-ordinators who, in turn, recruited 300 volunteers to provide free safety equipment checks on request. Since then, the scheme has developed considerably, the latest move being the appointment of a lifeboat sea safety officer (LSSO) at each station. These officers are often retired crew but always individuals who are interested in and knowledgeable about marine safety matters and who can talk to boat-owners, sport fishermen, sailing clubs or to anyone keen on improving their safety on or near water. Not every station has yet appointed a sea safety officer but their numbers are rising. The Institution also operates three sea safety trailers which are taken to gatherings of all kinds where there is likely to be an interested audience. These trailers contain a TV screen and a plasma screen and numerous publications on sea safety as well as promoting strongly the five top tips, viz:

1. Wear a lifejacket
2. Check your engine and fuel
3. Tell others where you are going
4. Carry some means of calling for help
5. Keep an eye on weather and tides.

Needless to say, the first of these, lifejackets and their maintenance, is the subject most discussed, this being one of the most successful areas of the whole initiative and the term "lifejacket clinic" is commonly heard. At these "clinics", lifejacket users are invited to bring along their own when they will be examined by the sea safety officer who will talk the owner through the steps of opening up the jacket and what to look for both inside and out. Some of those sessions attract many sailors who have never had the confidence to open up a lifejacket and the RNLI is well pleased with the success of this part of the campaign.

One of the logos, which it is hoped will strike a chord with sea-goers, is the outline of a lifejacket with, printed across it, the words "useless – unless worn".

On 2 January 2002, the first-ever RNLI lifeboats were introduced to the River Thames. Four stations now exist at Gravesend, Tower Pier, Chiswick Pier and Teddington, the first three using E-class Tiger Fast Response boats and the latter a traditional D-class inshore lifeboat. The Tiger-class boats are water-jet driven, capable of 40 knots and with no propellers, pose no problem regarding the pick-up of flotsam or, more importantly, injury to casualties in the water.

In the same year, hovercraft were introduced to cover shallow waters, sand banks and mud flats, the *Hurley Flyer*, a twin-engined VW turbo-diesel 1.9 being one of the current craft.

The latest innovation is the establishment on 2 April 2008 of the first inland ILB station in Scotland for 15 years. This station replaces a service hitherto run by the Marine and Coastguard Agency on Loch Ness and operates an Atlantic 75. The boat is based on the west shore of the loch and is capable of reaching either end of the area in the best possible time.

APPENDIX I

WORKING WITH HELICOPTERS

(Report Referred to in the Service of 10.1.98)

"DI Scotland
RNLI
Perth

Service Involving Night Winching – 10 January 1998

At about 2100 on the night of Saturday 10 January 1998 we located a missing canoeist with one arm lodged in his half submerged canoe. The position was 56°.8'N 5°19.25"W, no differential signal. Wind was S by W 3 to 4 and the sea was slight with no swell. Weather was fair and visibility was good with some moonlight.

Crewmember Dr Wilson, having examined the casualty, requested that Rescue 177, which was also involved in the search, should evacuate the casualty to hospital in Oban as his condition was very poor. This was passed to Rescue 177 together with the fact that the lifeboat required more sea room. Rescue 177 acknowledged and stood off while the lifeboat steamed at maximum speed to the south end of Balnagown Island such that the wind was 30° to port, and the requested speed of 10 knots was set. At this point the autopilot was engaged.

Twenty minutes later Shuna Island was abeam to port as the casualty and the winchman were winched clear and departed for Oban. On arrival at Oban the core temperature of the casualty was found to be 29°C. He has since made a full recovery.

During the entire operation it was possible to monitor the situation from the USP *(upper steering position),* and there is no doubt that the excellence of the steering system, together with the use of the autopilot, contributed to the safety and efficiency of the operation.

During the winchings, three in all, the helo was extremely close for considerable periods and I am sure that the pilot's task, difficult as it was, must have been rendered slightly less stressful by the accuracy of the lifeboat's course. It would not have been possible to steer by compass to anything like accuracy achieved, there being no visual references ahead, given the added distractions of navigation and command. All other crewmembers were heavily involved in dealing with the casualty.

Over the years we have only had two night helo exercises, both of which were aborted, though this was probably due to the difficulty experienced by the pilots working with a lifeboat as small as the Brede, and it was particularly pleasing, therefore, that this important service was accomplished without difficulty.

It became apparent at an early stage that, due to the proximity of the helo, any communications between the USP and the wheelhouse, the aft deck or the helo would be impossible and we would suggest that, in future, the flags be stored in the USP. As it was possible to look the pilot in the eye from the USP the use of a red flag to indicate a problem, such as running out of sea room, would be quick, simple and effective.

As mentioned elsewhere, we had problems with excessive reflections from the searchlights though, on this occasion, this was mitigated by the light nature of the night.

J P Maclean, coxswain, Oban Lifeboat
Copy to SHS Oban
16 January 1998"

APPENDIX II

LETTER FROM IAN MURRAY

(Letter referred to in the service of 10 January 1998)

109 Old Edinburgh Road
Inverness
IV2 3HT

16 January 1998

Dear Mr Macleod

I am writing you to express the gratitude felt by my family for
the promptness, expertise, patience and determination shown by
the Oban Life Boat crew on the evening of the 10th of January
when they rescued my son, Peter, and undoubtedly saved his
life, with but minutes to spare.

Words can not convey our thanks, and we would be pleased if
you would accept this cheque as a small tribute to the crew.

Please read this letter to them.

I am yours with thankfulness and respect,

Ian Maclean Murray

APPENDIX III

LETTER FROM JOHN HALLIDAY

(Letter referred to in service of 23 July 1996)

John A. Halliday

.Sc., F.R.C.S.(Ed.), F.R.C.S.(Eng.)

Telephone No. (01232) 668881

Fax No (01232) 667688

154 MALONE ROAD
BELFAST
BT9 5LJ

30.7.96.

Captain N. MacLeod,
Ceann A'Chreagain,
Pulpit Rock,
OBAN,
Argyll PA34 4LZ.

Dear Captain MacLeod,

On 23.7.96. Oban Lifeboat responded to the Mayday call from the motor yacht "Lady Blue" after the boat had sustained internal damage resulting in uncontained ingress of water.

My wife and I wish to thank the crew of the Oban lifeboat. As a member of the R.N.L.I. for some years, I knew that there would be a rapid response when the emergency was declared but I was very deeply impressed by the attitude of the lifeboat crew in taking every possible and successful step in not only preserving the safety of the crew of "Lady Blue" but also in ensuring that our boat was brought safely to port. The coxwain of the lifeboat accepted the increased inconvenience in escorting our boat, which was limited to four and a half knots, as far as Ardfern which he had established was the nearest site where adequate facilities existed to lift out the boat.

The three members of the crew (Colin, Jimmy and Harry) whom he put on board to assist in stemming the ingress of water, rapidly restored confidence to my wife and myself and showed unflagging good humour during the whole incident, in spite of the fact that they had just come off a previous emergency and must have been tired. Pat, the coxwain of the lifeboat, demonstrated superb boat handling on the occasions on which he had to come alongside "Lady Blue" and in the final docking.

My wife and I enclose a donation to the Oban Branch of the R.N.L.I. A more personal token to the crew of the lifeboat should arrive in the next two weeks.

Yours sincerely,

JOHN HALLIDAY

APPENDIX IV

OBAN LIFEBOATS 1972-2008

1972-82
Two MacLachlan-class 18-ft inshore lifeboats served the station in these years. Neither was named. Their numbers were A505 and A511.

1978-81
Watkin Williams (42-ft Watson-class) from the legacy of Miss ME Williams.

1981-82
Dorothy and Philip Constant (42-ft Watson-class), gift of Mr & Mrs Philip Constant.

1982-87
Ann Ritchie (33-ft Brede-class) gift of Mrs AA Ritchie.

1987-89
Merchant Navy (33-ft Brede-class) provided by the Merchant Navy Appeal.

1989-97
Nottinghamshire (33-ft Brede-class) provided from gifts of the Nottinghamshire Lifeboat Appeal 1982-84.

1997-
Mora Edith Macdonald (14-m Trent-class) from the legacy of Miss Mora Edith Macdonald together with those of Mrs Janet Boyd Finlay-Maclean, Mrs Harriet Elizabeth Willis Gaunt and Mrs Annie Thomson Hart.

APPENDIX V

Boats' Officers Past and Present

Ronnie MacKillop, coxswain	2004-
Jose Stuart, second coxswain	2008-
Jim Watson, mechanic	1997-
Keith Burnett, second mechanic	2000-
Pat Maclean, mechanic and coxswain	1978-1998
Douglas Craig, second coxswain	1989-2000
Lorne MacKechnie, deputy second coxswain	
and coxswain 1995-2004	1995-2004
David Graham, deputy second coxswain	
and second coxswain	1998-2004
Billy Forteith, deputy second coxswain	
and second coxswain	2001-2007

Station Officials Past and Present

Mike Robertson, chairman, hon press officer, DLA	2001-
Douglas Craig, hon sec/LOM	2001-
Colin Wilson, hon medical advisor/LMA	2000-
(now also divisional medical advisor for Scotland)	
Les Stewart, hon treasurer	1989-
David Graham, deputy launching authority	2004-
Billy Forteith, deputy launching authority	2007-
Lake Falconer, chairman,	1972-1997
deputy launching authority	1977-1977
Patrick Maclean, hon press officer, LSSO	2007-
Norman Budge, hon sec	1972-1973
Norman MacLeod, deputy launching authority,	1973-1973
hon sec	1973-2001
Gordon Murchison, hon medical advisor	1975-2000
Willie Melville, hon treasurer,	1972-1977
deputy launching authority	1989-2001
press officer	1994-2001
chairman	1997-2001
Donnie Currie, deputy launching authority	1973-1989
Gordon Murchison, hon medical advisor	1975-2000
Stewart Hunter, hon treasurer	1977-1979

Peter MacLeod, hon treasurer	1979-1989
Gordon Johnson, deputy launching authority	1994-2004
Malcolm Robertson, deputy launching authority	1996-2004

Fund-raising Guild Presidents Past and Present

Miss Isobel Black	1966-1979
Mrs Lesley MacPhail	1979-1984
Mrs Peigi Robertson	1984-1990
Mrs Anna Bevis	1990-1995
Mrs Shirley Allister	1996-1997
Mrs Marie-Claire MacDougall	1997-2005
Mrs Lorraine McCracken	2005-

Personnel Who Have Served on Oban Lifeboats Between May 1972 and December 2008

Name	"Day Job"
Burnett, Keith	Hydro-electric team manager
Campbell, Peter	Marine Engineer
Clark, Kenny	Engineer
Cleaver, Ian	Hotelier
Collins, Paul	NLB buoyage & helicopter co-ordinator
Cottier, Finlo	Marine scientist
Craig, Douglas	Boatbuilder
Docherty, John	Merchant seaman
Drummond, Gordon	Fish farm manager
Falconer, Lake	Solicitor
Forteith, Billy	Frozen foods company director
Glen, Robbie	NLB base assistant
Gordon, Ronnie	
Graham, David	Cycle-shop owner
Gunn, Kenny	Merchant seaman
Henry, Ian	Shipping accountant
Howard, Graeme	Surveyor
Hunter, Stuart	Building society manager
Huntingdon, Richard	Forester
Isaac, David	Lobster fisherman
Kirkham, Jim	Driver
Knowles, Euan	

Latham, Alan	Chef
Logan, Duncan	Assistant manager, NLB
MacDonald, James	Merchant seaman
MacKechnie, Lorne	Merchant seaman
MacKenzie, Sandy	Hotelier
MacKillop, Ronnie	Full-time coxswain
MacKinnon, Peter	Maintenance engineer
Maclean, Alasdair	Boatbuilder
Maclean, Patrick	Merchant seaman
MacLellan, Alick	Merchant seaman
MacQueen, Douglas	Marine engineer
MacTaggart, Barry	Hydro-electric team manager
Matheson, Donald	Floor-layer
McCuish, Ewan	Merchant seaman
McMaster, Harry	Merchant seaman
Melville, Willie	Bank manager
Murchison, Gordon	Doctor of medicine
Murchison, Kyle	Merchant seaman
Philips, Andy	Fisherman
Pirie, George	Distillery manager
Ritchie, Angus	Forestry Worker
Robertson, David	Hotelier
Robertson, Malcolm	Electronics engineer
Robertson, Mike	Solicitor
Russell, Craig	Ambulance man
Scott, Cyril	Tanker driver
Scott, Mark	Merchant seaman
Scott, Wilson	Chief steward, NLB
Smith, Tom	
Stevenson, Ian	Merchant seaman
Stewart, Donald	
Strachan, George	Merchant seaman
Stuart, Jose	Merchant seaman
Thomson, Sydney	Bosun, NLB
Turner, Gavin	Ambulance man
Watson, Jim	Full-time RNLI mechanic
Wilinski, Ryszard	Boatyard assistant
Wilson, Colin	Doctor of medicine

Wilson, John	Merchant seaman
Woolnough, James	Building contractor
Young, Ian	Schoolteacher

GLOSSARY

AWL	All Weather Lifeboat
Bends	De-compression sickness
Carrier	Channel carrying a radio signal
DLA	Deputy Launching Authority
EPIRB	Emergency position indicating radio beacon
Entonox	A gas used to dull pain
FAWGI	False alarm with good intent
Flashing-up	Stoking-up boilers
HMA	Honorary medical advisor (the station's doctor) now known as lifeboat medical advisor
Hon sec	Honorary secretary (a station's principal launching authority) now known as lifeboat operations manager
ILB	Inshore lifeboat
Insurance wire	Ships' mooring cable the absence of the use of which in heavy weather might prejudice an insurance claim
Jury	Temporary use
LSSO	Lifeboat Sea Safety Officer
Mayday	Internationally recognised signal for help (from the French *m'aidez* = help me)
Medivac	Medical evacuation
Pan-pan	Internationally-recognised signal for help but of lower urgency than mayday (from the French *"panne"* = breakdown)
SAR	Search and rescue
Shot line	Divers' marker buoy
Skittering	The slithering of an object across a smooth surface (Scots)
Transducer	Depth sensor
USP	Upper steering position
X, XP or Y boat	Small inflatable boat carried on most lifeboats

ACKNOWLEDGEMENTS

I have had invaluable assistance in the writing of this book from several people amongst whom there are a few I wish to mention specifically. When I was uncertain regarding technicalities or, indeed, any aspect of a "shout", I called upon the man who was nearly always "driving" – Pat Maclean. From Pat I received not only much accurate information but also great encouragement to keep going with the job.

The present coxswain, Ronnie MacKillop and station mechanic, Jim Watson, have also been most helpful in filling in some gaps and their patience with me was much appreciated. Mike Robertson, the present station chairman (a former fellow crew-member with whom I shared some exciting "shouts") and the crewmember who, thankfully, precipitated "the mutiny", has assisted me in many ways.

For most of the years which this book covers, shore-side affairs were in the hands of Norman MacLeod and, since his retiral, Douglas Craig, both of whom readily helped me where I required it.

When I have contacted anyone to whom Oban Lifeboat gave assistance, I have had the greatest of co-operation and ready agreement to name their boat where appropriate.

So far as photographs are concerned, everyone whose work I sought permission to reproduce were delighted to give it and have been credited in the captions. Where there is no credit given the photograph is either my own or I have been unable to trace the photographers – in this latter case I have taken the liberty to use their pictures in the hope that, having regard to the cause they are supporting, they would have given their agreement anyway. These photographers will almost certainly include The Oban Times, Brian Fair, Argyll and Islands Photography, David Graham and probably many others – my gratitude to all of them.

I must also put on record the invaluable advice I have had in the production of this book from Lynn Ashman, managing director of Indepenpress Publishing, and her colleagues Grace, Jacqueline, Linda and Kathryn.
Finally, this story would never have been written had there not been a lifeboat and a lifeboat crew at Oban. I have been privileged to serve on these boats and alongside their crews and I thank all of them for their fellowship.